Day Hike!

CENTRAL CASCADES

4th Edition

Day Hike!

CENTRAL CASCADES

4th Edition

Mike McQuaide

SASQUATCH BOOKS
SEATTLE

Printed in China

Published by Sasquatch Books
23 22 21 20 19   10 9 8 7 6 5 4 3 2 1

Cover photograph(s): Zachariah Schnepf | Cover design: Hillary Grant
Interior design: Andrew Fuller/Anna Goldstein | Interior photographs: Mike McQuaide.
Additional photos by Jim Kuresman (page 2), Thom Iverson (pages 6, 30, 128), Rob Casey
(pages 136, 217) and Laura Harrington (page 237) | Interior maps: Marlene Blair

Library of Congress Cataloging-in-Publication Data
Names: McQuaide, Mike, author.
Title: Day hike! Central Cascades / Mike McQuaide.
Description: Fourth edition | Seattle, WA : Sasquatch Books, 2019. | Includes
    index.
Identifiers: LCCN 2017041912 | ISBN 9781632171627 (paperback)
Subjects: LCSH: Hiking--Washington (State)--Guidebooks. | Hiking--Cascade
    Range--Guidebooks. | Trails--Washington (State)--Guidebooks. |
    Trails--Cascade Range--Guidebooks. | Washington (State)--Guidebooks. |
    Cascade Range--Guidebooks. | BISAC: SPORTS & RECREATION / Hiking. | SPORTS
    & RECREATION / General. | NATURE / Regional.
Classification: LCC GV199.42.W2 M37 2019 | DDC 796.5109797/5--dc23
LC record available at https://lccn.loc.gov/2017041912

ISBN: 978-1-63217-162-7

IMPORTANT NOTE: Please use common sense. No guidebook can act as a substitute for
experience, careful planning, the right equipment, and appropriate training. There is
inherent danger in all the activities described in this book, and readers must assume
full responsibility for their own actions and safety. Changing or unfavorable conditions
in weather, roads, trails, snow, waterways, and so forth cannot be anticipated by the
author or publisher, but should be considered by any outdoor participants. The author
and publisher will not be responsible for the safety of users of this guide, and neither
of them shall be liable or responsible for any legal liability, or any loss or damage or
physical injury of any kind, allegedly arising from any information herein.

Given the potential for changes to trail accessibility and hiking rules and regulations
post-publication, please check ahead for updates on contact information, parking
passes, and camping permits.

Sasquatch Books | 1904 Third Avenue, Suite 710 | Seattle, WA 98101
(206) 467-4300 | SasquatchBooks.com

CONTENTS

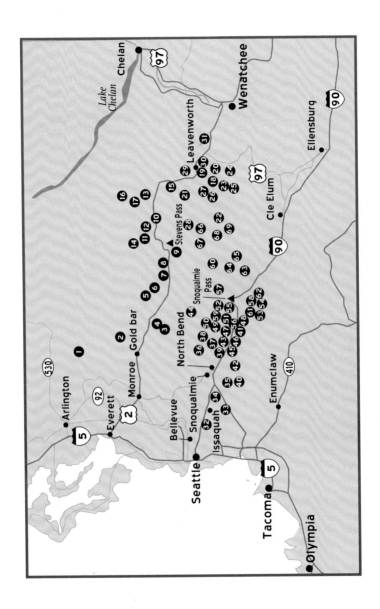

HIKES AT A GLANCE

EASY

NO.	HIKE NAME	RATING	BEST SEASON	KIDS	DOGS
6.	Barclay Lake	★★★	Spring, summer, fall	✔	✔
7.	Deception Falls Nature Trail	★★	Spring, summer, fall	✔	✔
8.	Iron Goat Trail	★★★★	Spring, summer, fall	✔	✔
10.	Bygone Byways Interpretive Trail	★★★	Summer, fall	✔	✔
15.	Penstock Trail	★★★	Spring, summer, fall	✔	✔
17.	Hidden Lake	★★★	Spring, summer, fall	✔	✔
19.	Leavenworth National Fish Hatchery	★★	Spring, summer, fall	✔	✔
28.	Icicle Gorge Trail	★★	Spring, summer, fall	✔	✔
29.	Ski Hill Loop	★★★	Spring, summer, fall	✔	✔
30.	Blackbird Island–Waterfront Park	★★	Spring, summer, fall	✔	✔
36.	Snoqualmie Falls	★★	Year-round	✔	
41.	John Wayne Pioneer Trail–Iron Horse State Park	★★★★	Spring, summer, fall	✔	✔
44.	Middle Fork Snoqualmie River	★★★	Spring, summer, fall	✔	✔
45.	Twin Falls	★★★	Year-round	✔	✔
46.	Weeks Falls	★★	Spring, summer, fall	✔	✔
53.	Asahel Curtis Nature Trail	★★★	Spring, summer, fall	✔	✔
56.	Franklin Falls–Wagon Road Loop	★★★	Spring, summer, fall	✔	✔
61.	Snoqualmie Tunnel	★★★	Summer, fall	✔	✔
63.	Gold Creek Pond	★★	Spring, summer, fall	✔	✔

MODERATE

NO.	HIKE NAME	RATING	BEST SEASON	KIDS	DOGS
4.	Bridal Veil Falls	★★★	Fall, winter, spring	✔	✔
5.	Heybrook Lookout	★★★	Spring, fall	✔	✔
9.	Grace Lakes	★★	Summer, fall	✔	✔
18.	Icicle Ridge	★★★	Spring, summer, fall	✔	✔

NO.	HIKE NAME	RATING	BEST SEASON	KIDS	DOGS
26.	Eightmile Lake	★ ★ ★ ★	Summer, fall		
31.	Peshastin Pinnacles	★ ★ ★	Spring, summer, fall		✔
32.	Cougar Mountain Wilderness Peak Loop	★ ★ ★	Year-round	✔	✔
33.	Squak Mountain	★ ★ ★	Year-round	✔	✔
37.	Little Si	★ ★ ★	Year-round	✔	✔
40.	Rattlesnake Ledge	★ ★ ★ ★	Spring, summer, fall	✔	✔
42.	Cedar Butte	★ ★ ★	Spring, summer, fall	✔	✔
47.	Dirty Harry's Balcony	★ ★ ★	Spring, summer, fall		✔
51.	Talapus–Olallie Lakes	★ ★ ★	Summer, fall	✔	✔
55.	Denny Creek–Melakwa Lake	★ ★ ★ ★	Summer, fall	✔	✔
57.	Snow Lake	★ ★ ★ ★	Summer, fall	✔	✔
58.	Lodge Lake	★ ★ ★	Summer, fall	✔	✔
62.	Mount Catherine	★ ★ ★	Summer, fall	✔	✔

MODERATELY DIFFICULT

NO.	HIKE NAME	RATING	BEST SEASON	KIDS	DOGS
2.	Wallace Falls	★ ★ ★ ★	Fall, winter, spring	✔	✔
12.	Merritt Lake	★ ★ ★ ★	Summer, fall	✔	✔
22.	Lake Stuart	★ ★ ★ ★ ★	Summer, fall		
35.	Rattlesnake Mountain (Snoqualmie Point to Grand Prospect)	★ ★ ★	Spring, summer, fall	✔	✔
39.	Talus Loop Trail	★ ★ ★	Spring, summer, fall	✔	✔
54.	Annette Lake	★ ★ ★ ★	Spring, summer, fall	✔	✔
59.	Commonwealth Basin–Red Pass	★ ★ ★ ★	Summer, fall	✔	✔
60.	Kendall Katwalk	★ ★ ★ ★ ★	Summer, fall		✔
68.	Longs Pass	★ ★ ★ ★ ★	Summer, fall	✔	✔

DIFFICULT

NO.	HIKE NAME	RATING	BEST SEASON	KIDS	DOGS
1.	Mount Pilchuck	★ ★ ★ ★	Summer, fall	✔	✔
3.	Lake Serene	★ ★ ★ ★	Summer, fall	✔	✔
13.	Round Mountain–Alpine Lookout	★ ★ ★ ★ ★	Summer, fall	✔	✔
14.	Nason Ridge	★ ★ ★ ★ ★	Summer, fall		✔
16.	Dirty Face Peak	★ ★ ★ ★	Summer, fall		✔

NO.	HIKE NAME	RATING	BEST SEASON	KIDS	DOGS
20.	Snow Lakes Trail	★★★★	Summer, fall		
23.	Colchuck Lake	★★★★★	Summer, fall		
27.	Lake Caroline–Windy Pass	★★★★★	Summer, fall		
29.	Ski Hill Loop	★★★	Spring, summer, fall	✔	✔
34.	West Tiger 3-2-1	★★★	Year-round		✔
38.	Mount Si	★★★★	Spring, summer, fall		✔
48.	McClellan Butte	★★★★	Summer, fall		✔
49.	Ira Spring Trail	★★★★★	Spring, summer, fall		✔
50.	Mason Lake–Mount Defiance	★★★★★	Spring, summer, fall	✔	✔
64.	Rachel Lake	★★★★	Summer, fall	✔	✔
65.	Rampart Ridge–Alta Mountain	★★★★★	Summer, fall		✔
66.	Paddy-Go-Easy Pass	★★★★	Summer, fall		✔
67.	Cathedral Rock	★★★★	Summer, fall		✔
69.	Ingalls Way Trail	★★★★★	Summer, fall		✔

EXTREME

NO.	HIKE NAME	RATING	BEST SEASON	KIDS	DOGS
11.	Rock Mountain	★★★★	Summer, fall		✔
21.	Fourth of July Creek	★★★★	Spring, summer, fall		✔
24.	Little Annapurna	★★★★★	Summer, fall		
25.	The Enchantments	★★★★★	Summer, fall		
43.	Mailbox Peak	★★★★	Spring, summer, fall		✔
52.	Granite Mountain	★★★★★	Summer, fall		✔

ACKNOWLEDGMENTS

A huge shout-out of thanks, gratitude, and appreciation to the following individuals and organizations for offering their support, expertise, and friendship: Bud Hardwick, Jim Kuresman, Doug McKeever, Tim Schultz, Frank Schultz, Paul Ricci, Rick Lingbloom, the Steeles, Margaret Gerard, Washington Trails Association, the *Seattle Times*, and of course, the fine people at Sasquatch Books.

THE CENTRAL CASCADES

The Cascade Mountains stretch all the way from the Fraser River in lower British Columbia south to Northern California. For the purposes of this book, the Central Cascades are defined as that section of the range easily accessed from Highway 2 and Interstate 90. Basically, the corridors from Everett to Leavenworth, and Seattle to Cle Elum. Also included is Mount Pilchuk, because of its prominence and proximity to Everett.

From soaking wet, deep valley rain forests to high and dry alpine wonderlands, the Central Cascades offer the gamut of hiking experiences. There are short, riverside walks to places such as Twin Falls, where the Snoqualmie River plunges 150 feet in a misty explosion below, as well as mountaintop vistas more than a mile-and-a-half high such as Little Annapurna where, on clear days, you'll swear you can see the four corners of Washington State—and everything in between. (Take Rachel Lake and Rampart Ridge, for instance; they've got a bit of both.)

Though both Highway 2 and Interstate 90 trend toward the south a bit, they run west to east, more or less. Thus, as you drive either across the state, you can watch as the terrain undergoes incredible and awe-inspiring changes—from the deep evergreen fir and cedar forests, lingering mountain snow, and buckets of rain on the west side to the east side's sunny days, dry pine forests, and penchant for triple digit temperatures. That east-west diversity is especially dramatic along Highway 2, because it's farther north and climbs higher than Interstate 90; Stevens Pass tops out at 4,061 feet, Snoqualmie Pass at 3,022 feet. As such, both highways are springboards for a smorgasbord of wildly diverse hiking experiences.

The west side is known for the wet face it tends to put on things. Clouds rolling in from the west tend to dump most of their moisture on the west side of the Cascade crest—elevation, about 3,000 to 5,000 feet—before they ever make it to the east side. From November to April, at elevations above 3,000 feet or so, this usually means snow.

The rest of the year those clouds offer much in the way of rain, showers, drizzle, fog, and precip. (From mid-July to the end of August, they do give it a rest.) All that moisture means you'll come across more snow on the west side. Not surprisingly, waterfalls—that's why they're called the Cascade Mountains after all—and water, in general, are more plentiful on the west side, too.

With the clouds mostly rained and snowed out by the time they cross the crest, the east side enjoys less snow and rain than the west, and more sunny days. Most years, mountain trails on the east sides of Snoqualmie and Stevens Passes are clear of snow weeks earlier than those on the west.

Common trees in the Central Cascades include western red cedar, western hemlock, Douglas fir, and Pacific silver fir, with the east side of the Cascades boasting ponderosa pine, Engelmann spruce, and subalpine and western larch. The Enchantment Lakes is world-famous for its larch, which in fall turn a brilliant yellow-gold.

Being a day-hiking guide, this book won't pretend to be a comprehensive guide to Northwest flora and fauna; animal-wise and plant-wise, the species are too numerous to catalog, but some of the common critters worth mentioning include bald eagle, osprey, black bear, Roosevelt elk, mountain lion, hoary marmot, pika, mountain goat, American dipper, raven, and, on the east side, the occasional rattlesnake. Among the plants you're likely to see are trillium, Indian paintbrush, subalpine lupine, mountain heather, columbine, devil's club, huckleberry, blueberry, and countless varieties of fungi and algae.

Alpine Lakes Wilderness

Most of the hiking trails in this book are on land in the Mount Baker–Snoqualmie or Okanogan-Wenatchee National Forests. Although not national park land, many trails are in the Alpine Lakes Wilderness, a spectacular 414,710-acre mountain and forest wonderland sprinkled with nearly 700 lakes, which is comanaged by both forest agencies. Created in 1976, the wilderness is easily accessed at numerous points along Interstate 90 and Highway 2, and about half the state's population lives within an hour of Alpine Lakes Wilderness. As such, solitude is not always easy to find. But weekday visits dramatically improve your chances. Day permits are required for hiking the Alpine Lakes Wilderness; they're free and are available at trailheads.

Alpine Lakes Wilderness trails range from easy west-side jaunts to places such as Denny Creek near Snoqualmie Pass to otherworldly moonscapes such as the hard-to-get-to, high-elevation Enchantment Lakes Basin, just outside Leavenworth.

Speaking of Leavenworth, this Bavarian-themed town makes an excellent not-too-far-away, eastside getaway that's right on the edge of some spectacular hiking. Icicle Road, mere minutes from your favorite espresso joint, offers what seems like dozens of world-class hiking opportunities—Icicle Ridge, Lake Caroline–Windy Pass, Little Annapurna, the Enchantments, Lake Stuart, and more. When it comes to hiking, Leavenworth is hard to beat.

Fees

Hiking is free on national forest trails, but parking isn't. To park at most of the trailheads in this book (unless the description says otherwise), day hikers need a Northwest Forest Pass. Forest passes cost $5 for a daily pass, $30 for an annual. They're available at National Forest Ranger stations, REI stores and various retail outlets throughout the Puget Sound region, and online at www.fs.fed.us.

Another option is to buy an America the Beautiful Pass ($80 annually), good for entry at any federal site (e.g. national parks, national forests, etc.). If you regularly visit national parks and use forest-service trailheads, it's a great deal. For those 62 and older, the Interagency Senior Pass is an $80 lifetime pass that offers the same privileges. Both passes are available at the same outlets listed above and from www.nps.gov.

In addition, state parks now require a Discover Pass. It costs $10 for a daily pass, $30 for an annual, and is available at various retail outlets and online at www.discoverpass.wa.gov.

USING THIS GUIDE

The beginning of each trail description is intended to give you quick information that can help you decide whether the specific day hike is one that interests you. Here's what you'll find:

Trail Number & Name

Trails are numbered in this guide following a geographical order; see the Trail Overview Map on page vii for general location. Trail names usually reflect those names used by the national forest service and/or other land managers.

Overall Rating

Since it's so subjective, assigning an overall rating to a hike can be a difficult task because of the different-strokes-for-different-folks phenomenon. That said, because I hiked all the trails and have opinions about which ones I liked, which ones I liked a lot, which ones I loved, and which ones I loved and never wanted to leave, assigning ratings wasn't that hard.

In order for the ratings to make sense to you, it'd probably be of some help if I explained what kinds of things turn my trekking poles up to 11 and, thus, were likely to make me rate a particular trail higher than another.

In general, trails in dense forest with no mountain vistas rate lower than those with mountain views. I love the dense Northwest forests as much as anyone, but because this is a book about the Central Cascade Mountains, the trails with the mountain vistas are the ones that rate the highest. Water features, whether rushing rivers, cascading waterfalls, or peaceful alpine lakes, raise a trail's rating, as do wildflower meadows. Lack of crowds is a plus, too.

Trails that rate the highest are those that fire on all cylinders. For example, you might pass through dense woods, cross meadows splashed with Indian paintbrush and myriad wildflowers, climb to an alpine environment where you're surrounded by mountains, ridges, and glaciers, and, finally, after a short rock scramble, you reach an old fire lookout from which the views are out of this world. Granite Mountain (Hike 52) is a good example.

With the above in mind, trails are rated from one to five, with five reserved for the most spectacular trails. (Truthfully, though, I don't think I included any ones; a one rating of anything seems a bit pathetic.)

★ This hike is worth taking, even with your in-laws.

★★ Expect to discover socially and culturally redeeming values on this hike. Or, at least, very fine scenery.

★★★ You would be willing to get up before sunrise to take this hike, even if you binge-watched *Game of Thrones* the night before.

★★★★ Here is the Häagen-Dazs of hikes; if you don't like ice cream, a hike with this rating will give more pleasure than any favorite comfort food.

★★★★★ The aesthetic and physical rewards are so great that hikes given this rating are forbidden by most conservative religions.

Distance

These are the best estimates I could come up with. Determining distances on trails is difficult as maps are not always accurate and are often at odds with trail signs and other maps.

Hiking Time

This is an estimate of the time it takes the average hiker to walk the trail, round-trip. Since none of us are average hikers, feel free to ignore this entry. For the most part, however, the pace on the trail is calculated at 2 to 3 miles per hour, depending on how flat or steep a trail is.

Elevation Gain

This is the trail's cumulative elevation gain. Not all of it will be gained on the way to your destination. Some trails actually lose elevation on the way out and gain it on the return, or alternately gain and lose elevation along the way. The certainty is that on a round-trip hike, you always gain the same amount of elevation that you lose.

High Point
This is the highest point above sea level you'll reach on the hike.

Difficulty Level
Here's where you'll find how much effort you'll be expending on a particular trail. Hills, how primitive a trail is, length, and elevation gain were all taken into consideration in rating a trail. Similar to the overall rating, this is very subjective. And as with the hiking times, the difficulty of individual hikes was rated conservatively.

Trail difficulty is rated from one to five, with five being reserved for hikers with high endurance seeking the greatest challenge.

- ♦ Easy: Few, if any, hills; generally between 1 and 4 miles, round-trip; suitable for families with small children.

- ♦♦ Moderate: Longer, gently graded hills; generally 4 to 6 miles long, round-trip.

- ♦♦♦ Moderately Difficult: Steeper grades; elevation changes greater than about 1,000 feet; between 6 and 9 miles long, round-trip.

- ♦♦♦♦ Difficult: Sustained, steep climbs of at least 1 mile; elevation gain and loss greater than 1,500 feet; usually more than 9 miles long, round-trip.

- ♦♦♦♦♦ Extreme: Sustained steep climbs; distances greater than 10 miles, round-trip. These trails are high on the lung-busting, thigh-burning, knee-crunching scale and will put your hiking skills to the test.

Best Season
Here's our recommendation for the best time of year to take any given hike. Trails that are open throughout the year or make good three-season hikes will be noted here.

Permits/Contact

This entry will tell you whether you need a Northwest Forest Pass and which land manager to contact for more information.

Maps

The two most popular types of maps, United States Geological Survey (USGS) "quads" and Green Trails, are listed for each hike where applicable.

Each hike in this book includes a trail map of the route, featuring parking and trailhead, alternate routes, direction, elevation profile, and more. Our maps are based most often on USGS; use the legend on the opposite page.

Trail Notes

Look here for a quick guide to trail regulations and features: leashed dogs okay; off-leash dogs okay; no dogs; kid-friendly; great views; bikes allowed; plus other quirky info.

After the at-a-glance overview of each hike, you'll then find detailed descriptions:

The Hike

This section conveys the feel of the trail in a few sentences; it includes the type of trail and whether the views are jaw-dropping or just simply grand.

Getting There

Here's where you'll find driving directions to the trailhead from the nearest major highway. The trailhead elevation is also included.

The main access highways for all but one of these hikes are Interstate 90 (Mountains to Sound Greenway) and Highway 2 (Stevens Pass Greenway). I-90 heads east from Seattle and most of the I-90–accessed trails in this book are found between mileposts 15 and 85, ranging from 15 to 85 miles east of Seattle.

Highway 2 heads east from Everett, about 30 miles north of Seattle, and most of the Highway 2-accessed hikes are between mileposts 28 and 99 (from 28 to 99 miles east of Everett).

The Trail

Here's the blow-by-blow, mile-by-mile description of each trail. Along with route descriptions, you'll find what to look forward to—awesome views, killer uphills, easy-to-miss turnoffs, and so forth. Distances to selected intersections and landmarks along the way are also included.

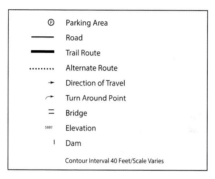

Ⓟ	Parking Area
——	Road
▬▬	Trail Route
··········	Alternate Route
→	Direction of Travel
↱	Turn Around Point
=	Bridge
5880'	Elevation
I	Dam
	Contour Interval 40 Feet/Scale Varies

Going Farther

In this section, you can learn about good options for extending the hike along the same trail. Interesting side trips can be found here, too. And if there's a nearby campground that could get you on the trail sooner, it also will be mentioned. Not every hike includes this section.

BE CAREFUL

Admittedly, a 6-mile round-trip day hike to Snow Lake isn't quite the same undertaking as a 10-day backpacking trip on the Pacific Crest Trail. Still, day hiking does require some preparation. Along with common sense, day hikers need to take along certain items in the event of accident or injury. They should also take along some knowledge about the weather they're likely to encounter, as well as the terrain and its inhabitants.

The Ten Essentials

No matter the distance or difficulty of the hike, always carry the Ten Essentials in your pack.

- A topographic **map** of the area.
- A **compass**, and the ability to use it in conjunction with the map. Portable GPS units are excellent aids to navigation, but can't always be depended on in areas of heavy tree cover. Also, they require batteries, which can fail.
- **Extra clothing**, consisting of a top and bottom insulating layer and a waterproof and windproof top layer. A hat or cap is also a necessity.
- A one-day supply of **water** and **extra food** that requires no cooking. Energy bars, jerky, or dried fruits work well.
- Carry a **flashlight** with extra batteries and bulbs; a headlamp is a good option. Many of these lights have spare bulbs built-in. Lithium batteries, though more expensive, make excellent spares because of their long shelf-life.
- Excellent **first-aid kits** that come already assembled are available on the market. Make sure your kit includes wraps for sprains and some kind of blister treatment.
- **Matches** in a waterproof case are recommended over butane lighters, as both altitude and temperature can affect a lighter's performance.
- Candles work well as a **fire starter**, along with a variety of lightweight commercial products.

- A **pocketknife** is an indispensable tool.
- **Sunglasses** and **sunscreen** are important, especially at high altitudes or when the ground is snow-covered.

In addition to these items, most day hikers heading into the mountains in the summer months never hit the trail without bug repellent. A loud emergency whistle is a worthy consideration, too. Consider using trekking poles or a walking stick to assist with balance and reduce the stress on your knees, ankles, and back.

Water

Dehydration is one of the most common ailments that day hikers face. Never head out on the trail without carrying at least a quart of clean water per person. As stated elsewhere in this book, the west side of the Cascades is a very wet place, so finding water to filter or treat before drinking shouldn't be a problem. East of Stevens and Snoqualmie Passes, however, it can be a different story, especially in high summer. On trails where creeks and lakes are scarce and finding water might be a problem, it's usually mentioned in the trail description.

Because of the prevalence of *Giardia lamblia*, a nasty parasite that lives in creeks, rivers, and streams, drinking untreated water is a bad idea. If you must drink from a creek or lake, treat the water with iodine tablets, or use a lightweight filter or water purification system. Water treatment systems for backcountry travelers have undergone a revolution in recent years. Pumps, straws, gravitational reservoirs, and even ultraviolet lights are being used to treat water; all have their pluses and minuses. Pick something and use it.

Weather

Northwest weather can be highly unpredictable, especially at higher elevations. An old salt once told me that above 5,000 feet, there's the potential for winter every single day of the year. He knew what he spoke of, too, for he told me this on a summer night when we were huddled in a tent at the toe of Mount Baker's Easton Glacier during a raging snowstorm blowing 30 mph winds. Then again, some summer days, especially on the warmer east side, can have temps over 100 degrees F and be so sunny and bright that sunstroke is a concern.

Of course, all elevations offer the potential for rain, and where there's rain, wind, and cool temperatures, hypothermia is a real threat. Waterproof, windproof gear can be lifesaving in such situations. Treat hypothermia by doing the following: Get the person out of the rain, cold, and wind immediately. Remove all wet clothing. Because hypothermia victims are often dehydrated, give them plenty of fluids to drink. Get them indoors as soon as possible, but remember that gradual rewarming of the victim is advisable. Rewarming that is too abrupt can strain the hypothermic person's heart. To prevent hypothermia, know the weather conditions and forecast, and always carry extra clothes.

To be safe, always call the appropriate land manager or check their websites for the latest trail conditions, including snow levels.

Flora & Fauna

For the most part, the animals and plants of the Cascades are harmless. The most common danger might be an encounter with a black bear or, in rare instances, a cougar. On the east side, rattlesnakes are sometimes also seen.

Day hikers needn't fear black bears, but do realize these are wild animals that can cause serious injury if provoked. While there are few (if any) grizzly bears to worry about, research indicates that a black bear attack, although extremely rare, may lead more often to a fatality.

If you do encounter a bear, cougar, or rattlesnake, heed the following advice from the Department of Fish and Wildlife:

BEAR: Give the bear plenty of room to get away. Never get between a cub and its mother. Avoid eye contact but speak softly to the bear while backing away from it. Try not to show fear and don't turn your back on a bear. If you can't get away from it, clap your hands or yell in an effort to scare it away. If the bear becomes aggressive, fight back using anything at your disposal. Should the attack continue, curl up in a ball or lay down on your stomach and play dead.

COUGAR: Don't take your eyes off the cougar. Make yourself appear big by raising your arms above your head, open your jacket if you're wearing one, and wave a stick above your head. If the cougar approaches, yell and throw rocks, sticks, or anything you can get your hands on. In the event of an attack, fight back aggressively.

RATTLESNAKE: Most of the time, if you come across a rattlesnake, it will slither away, but if not, give it plenty of room—about 10 feet—and walk around it. Rattlers can strike up to four feet, and although sometimes their bites are dry, it's not the type of thing that you should take a chance with. If bitten, seek medical treatment as soon as possible.

Less dangerous, but more common hazards to day hikers include stinging and biting pests such as yellow jackets, particularly in late summer and early fall; and black flies, mosquitoes, and deer flies. Liberal doses of insect repellent can take care of the mosquitoes and deer flies, but probably won't keep those pesky yellow jackets away.

Poison oak and ivy grow in some areas of the Cascades, mostly in sunny, dry areas. A more common plant pest is stinging nettle, which grows in profusion along many trails.

Etiquette/Ethics

To protect this wonderful landscape so that users in future generations can enjoy it just as much as you, please follow a few simple rules. Stay on established trails, don't cut switchbacks, and stay off sensitive areas. Leave no trace, pack out your trash, and respect other trail users. And because you're having such a great time using Washington's trails, why not volunteer your services by lending a hand on a trail building or repair project? Hit the trails! ■

FOOTHILLS

---

1. Mount Pilchuck

RATING	DISTANCE	HIKING TIME
★★★★☆	6.0 miles round-trip	4 hours
ELEVATION GAIN	HIGH POINT	DIFFICULTY
2,300 feet	5,340 feet	◆◆◆◆
BEST SEASON		
Jan Feb Mar Apr May Jun **Jul Aug Sep Oct** Nov Dec		

The Hike

In the same way that Mount Si is Seattle's closest Cascade-esque mountain and hiking hot spot, Mount Pilchuck fills that role for the Everett area. Fewer than 20 miles by air from downtown Everett, Mount Pilchuck is that prominent pyramid in the foreground when you look east from pretty much anywhere near Everett. A meticulously maintained fire lookout on top makes this an especially cool destination.

The lookout on Mount Pilchuck

Getting There

From the Mountain Loop Highway in Granite Falls, drive east about 12 miles to Mount Pilchuck Road (Forest Road 42). Turn right and continue for 7 miles to the trailhead parking lot. Elevation: 3,100 feet.

The Trail

Interesting tidbits abound on this trail. For example, did you know there was a ski area on this mountain from 1957 to 1980? Or that the mountain's first lookout cabin was built in 1919, only to be replaced in 1938? Or that the lookout is on the National Historic Building Register and is maintained by the Everett branch of The Mountaineers? Well, now you do.

From the trailhead, start by climbing steeply (and somewhat relentlessly) through stately old-growth forest, switchbacking as you go. Enter Mount Pilchuck State Park after about a quarter-mile; an old sign confirms you're on the right path. In about a half mile the trail passes through a clear-cut area that offers a hint of the views that will eventually be had in great abundance. After another forested stretch, the trail offers hints of something else that's to come: boulder fields that dominate much of the rest of the way.

At **1.6** miles reach a flat shoulder area that features impressive views to the North Cascades. Duck back into forest for about a quarter mile, and when you next emerge into the open, you're in a land of craggy cliffs and huge, exposed rock slabs. Pilchuck's rocky upper

PERMITS/CONTACT
Northwest Forest Pass required/Mount Baker–Snoqualmie National Forest, Verlot Public Service Center, (360) 691-7791, Mount Pilchuck State Park, (360) 793-0420

MAPS
USGS Verlot; Green Trails Granite Falls 109

TRAIL NOTES
Leashed dogs okay; kid-friendly; spectacular views; historic lookout building—last few feet to the lookout building can be tricky

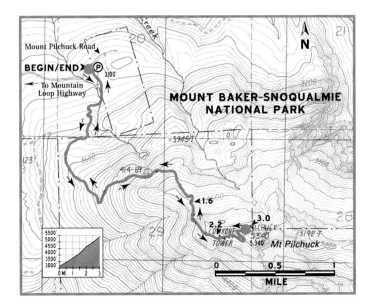

reaches loom high above, seemingly directly overhead. Give a good squint and you'll spot the fire lookout. At **2.2** miles the trail contours along the mountain's west and south sides, opening up views of Mount Rainier and the Olympic Mountains beyond.

Continue climbing through a mix of boulder field and forest until you reach the top (5,340 feet), at **3.0** miles. The final 25 feet to the lookout is a scramble up giant boulders and a short climb up a ladder. Views are all-encompassing—a string of volcanoes from Rainier to Glacier to Baker, the Olympics, and all of North Puget Sound. Spread throughout is the plethora of lowland towns, burgs, villages, and hamlets.

Return the same way, reminding yourself to step carefully on the rocky sections; you've only got one pair of ankles and knees. ■

2. Wallace Falls

RATING	DISTANCE	HIKING TIME
★★★★ ☆	6.6 miles round-trip	4 hours
ELEVATION GAIN	**HIGH POINT**	**DIFFICULTY**
1,350 feet	1,650 feet	◆ ◆ ◆ ◇ ◇

BEST SEASON											
Jan	Feb	Mar	Apr	May	Jun	Jul	Aug	Sep	Oct	Nov	Dec

The Hike

The park's 265-foot plunging horsetail of water is the star attraction on this trail, and if you're ever curious as to how popular waterfalls are, visit this trail on a sunny weekend. This is one reason to visit when the weather is crummy. The other is that waterfalls are always more impressive during the wet months. Another plus for the kiddies: the best views of the falls are actually fairly low.

Getting There

Go east on Highway 2 to the town of Gold Bar, just before milepost 28, about 14 miles east of Everett. Turn left on First Street and follow signs for about 2 miles to Wallace Falls State Park. Elevation: 350 feet.

PERMITS/CONTACT
Discover Pass required/Wallace Falls State Park, (360) 793-0420

MAPS
USGS Wallace Lake, Gold Bar; Green Trails Index 142

TRAIL NOTES
Leashed dogs okay; kid-friendly; great valley views; 265-foot waterfall

Plunging Wallace Falls makes quite a splash

The Trail

Although the main 265-foot-high waterfall that is visible from Highway 2 is perhaps the most impressive, it is not the only one in Wallace Falls State Park. Within park boundaries, the Wallace River drops 800 feet in less than a half-mile, creating nine falls that drop more than 50 feet. The 2.9-mile, one-way Woody Trail offers several opportunities to take in these breathtaking waterfalls.

Both the river and the falls are named after Sarah Kwayaylsh, whose last name was twisted into "Wallace" by English speakers. The trailhead kiosk states that in the late 1800s she was a "strong spirited woman of the Skykomish Indian Tribe who homesteaded between Gold Bar and Startup."

After giving the trailhead map kiosk a once-over, sign the register and be on your way, heading up the obvious trail. After passing below some daunting, buzzing, zapping, not-exactly-wilderness-feeling power lines, enter the forest. The trail is at times rough and slippery (aren't we all, really); at **0.5** mile go right on the signed Woody Trail, passing through a bike barricade as you do. (If, for a variation, you decide to return via the Railroad Grade Trail, which is on the left, here's where you'll return to the main trail.)

After a mini descent, the trail crosses a bridge, and after a short climb it cozies up to the Wallace River. Rocks and roots along the trail here will keep you on your toes, especially on the way back. At **1.5** miles take note of—but don't take—the Railroad Grade Trail, which intersects to the left. On the way back you can take a right here to add about a mile of easier grade and not-quite-so-primitive walking on your return.

A third of a mile farther, near a pleasant picnic shelter, catch the first really good glimpse of the falls. For even better views continue switchbacking up the trail, and at **2.3** miles you'll find yourself

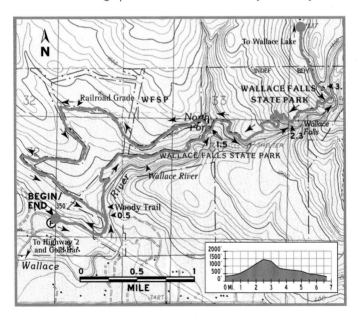

gaping and gawking at the tumbling rumble of water. Wallace Falls is one of the highest single-plunge cataracts in the Northwest. Although Snoqualmie Falls launches a greater volume of water from its rock cliffs, that world-renowned waterfall is only 5 feet higher than Wallace.

Continue a steep half-mile to another viewpoint, this one boasting views to the Skykomish Valley and the Olympic Mountains. At **3.3** miles reach the last of the four viewpoints, which offers two impressive plungers, even if they're much smaller than the main falls. Return the same way until you get to the "Railroad Grade" sign. Go right if you want a less steep, less primitive return.

Going Farther

In 2007, through the efforts of Washington Trails Association (WTA), Landmark Volunteers, and AmeriCorps, the 2.5-mile Greg Ball Trail to Wallace Lake opened. Named in honor of Greg Ball, who started WTA's trail maintenance program and who died in 2004, the well-signed trail starts at the end of the Railroad Grade Trail where it intersects with the Woody Trail. ■

3. Lake Serene

RATING	DISTANCE	HIKING TIME
★★★★☆	7.2 miles round-trip	3 hours
ELEVATION GAIN	**HIGH POINT**	**DIFFICULTY**
2,300 feet	2,560 feet	◆◆◆◆◇

BEST SEASON
Jan Feb Mar Apr May **Jun Jul Aug Sep Oct Nov** Dec

The Hike

Although this hike tops out at only 2,560 feet, for some reason it feels like you're much higher in the alpine. Whistling marmots add to the effect. Hop atop Lunch Rock and enjoy a "serenity now" moment while contemplating the cerulean, otherworldly waters of Lake Serene. That is, when you're not scanning the 3,500-foot rock wall on Mount Index, which looks close enough to touch. This is also the trailhead for the Bridal Veil Falls Trail (Hike 4).

Getting There

Head east on Highway 2 to milepost 35.2, about 21 miles east of Monroe. Turn right onto Mount Index Road (Forest Road 6020), and in 0.3 mile turn right at a fork onto FR 6020-109. The trailhead parking lot is just ahead. Elevation: 600 feet.

PERMITS/CONTACT
Northwest Forest Pass required/Mount Baker–Snoqualmie National Forest, Skykomish Ranger District, (360) 677-2414

MAPS
USGS Index; Green Trails Index 142

TRAIL NOTES
Leashed dogs okay; kid-friendly; great lake and Mount Index views

Lunch Rock by the cerulean waters of Lake Serene

The Trail

Although it's called Lake Serene, on summer weekends this trail is anything but, so leave early in the a.m. Or, better yet, go during the week if you can. From behind the trailhead kiosk, follow the old logging road as it takes its time leading you into the second-growth forest and up away from sea level. But don't fall for it: while the first half of the trail is gentle, the second half makes up for it in a hurry, mostly via a series of spiffy wood staircases that were built in the late 1990s when the trail was vastly improved.

At about **1.6** miles—shortly after bearing right at an unmarked fork, then left at a marked one—reach the intersection with the Bridal Veil Falls Trail. Go left and shortly after ducking into older, denser, and darker forest, cross Bridal Veil Creek over a bridge, and follow your ears for partially obstructed views of the plunging water.

Once across the bridge, begin climbing in earnest to the tune of 1,400 feet in about 2 miles and twenty-three switchbacks.

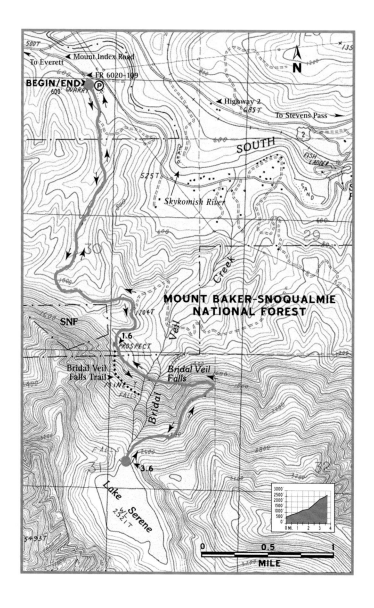

To Everett
Mount Index Road
FR 6020-109
BEGIN/END
QUARRY
P
500T
600
600
600
N
Highway 2
685T
To Stevens Pass
2
SOUTH
FISH
LADDER
525T
Skykomish River
SAND
600
600
29
Creek
1000
MOUNT BAKER-SNOQUALMIE
NATIONAL FOREST
1204T
1600
SNF
1.6
PROSPECT
Bridal Veil
Falls Trail
FALLS
Bridal Veil
Falls
1600
Bridal
Veil
1600
1200
3.6
1800
1600
FALLS
31
32
1600
Lake
Serene
2521T
3000'
2500'
2000'
1500'
1000'
500'
0'
0 Mi. 1   2   3   4
54,937
0   0.5   1
MILE

Marvel at, thank, and maybe even kneel down and kiss the wood stairs that make this climb easier and much safer than it would be otherwise. From time to time views open up to the north revealing the Skykomish River valley below and rocky walls and ridges high across the valley. If you look really close, you'll see the Heybrook Lookout (Hike 5), itself a neat day-hiking destination.

At **3.6** miles reach the cliff-lined lake and find yourself no doubt gaping in wonder at the 3,500-foot rock wall of Mount Index that rises high above the cerulean water like a series of mega shark fins. When driving east from Gold Bar on Highway 2, Mount Index is the one that dominates the sky, and here it is, large and certainly in charge. Follow boardwalks along the lake to various viewpoints, including one at the top of Bridal Veil Falls (Lake Serene is its source). Enjoy some lunch atop aptly named Lunch Rock, a giant glacier-scoured boulder at water's edge. Bask in the sun and enjoy the sights. This is an amazing place.

Return the same way.

Going Farther

The Bridal Veil Falls Trail uses the same trailhead as this trail. Camping is available at Money Creek Campground, just off Highway 2, near milepost 45. ■

4. Bridal Veil Falls

RATING	DISTANCE	HIKING TIME
★★★ ☆☆	4.2 miles round-trip	2 hours

ELEVATION GAIN	HIGH POINT	DIFFICULTY
1,000 feet	1,600 feet	♦♦ ◇◇◇

BEST SEASON
Jan Feb Mar Apr May Jun Jul Aug Sep Oct Nov Dec

The Hike

Spectacular when seen from Highway 2, Bridal Veil Falls is even more impressive from up close as it tumbles down 100 feet from a rock cliff almost directly overhead. Watch your step, though; sections of this trail are rocky, always wet, and potentially very slippery. And, of course, if you're not careful, the falls themselves make no bones about sweeping you down into the Skykomish Valley. This is also the trailhead for the Lake Serene Trail (Hike 3).

Getting There

Head east on Highway 2 to milepost 35.2, about 21 miles east of Monroe. Turn right onto Mount Index Road (Forest Road 6020), and in 0.3 mile turn right at a fork onto FR 6020-109. The trailhead parking lot is just ahead. Elevation: 600 feet.

PERMITS/CONTACT
Northwest Forest Pass required/Mount Baker–Snoqualmie National Forest,
Skykomish Ranger District, (360) 677-2414

MAPS
USGS Index; Green Trails Index 142

TRAIL NOTES
Leashed dogs okay; kid-friendly—but hold their hands, especially near the falls

Spectacular falls can be spectacularly slippery

The Trail

Let it be known that with two popular trails sharing the same trailhead, this can be a crowded place on weekends. Luckily, the times of the year when the most water is pouring down the falls—that is, when the falls are the most impressive—is when most people are inside trying to stay warm and dry. Find the trail (actually an old logging road at first) behind the kiosk map and follow as it climbs gradually

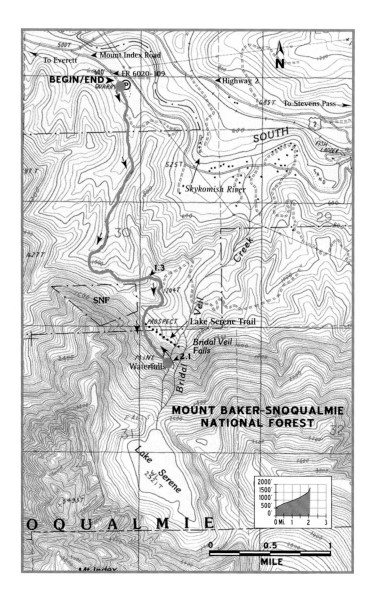

through second-growth forest. At about **1.3** miles bear right where the trail widens and in a few hundred yards reaches a signed intersection with the Lake Serene Trail. Turn right, following the sign for Bridal Veil Falls. Just ahead, take a moment to examine the remains of and artifacts from an old prospector's cabin, a leftover from the days of yore when copper, and even gold and silver, were mined in these here hills.

The trail climbs steeply through forest for about a quarter-mile, including one stretch via some wood stairs that look like a giant ladder leaning against the hillside. The trail then traverses the hillside for a few hundred muddy yet rocky yards (watch your step!) in which the trees open up to reveal expansive views of the Skykomish River valley, Heybrook Ridge (including the lookout), and more.

After one last short climb, the trail reaches the falls at **2.1** miles. You're basically between two hundred-foot-high cataracts here—one that's plunging and streaking down a rock face in front of you, and another that's falling a hundred feet or more off the ledge behind you. It's misty and wet and slippery up here, so admire the falls from a safe position—don't see how close you can get to the edge just to get a better look.

Return the same way. ■

5. Heybrook Lookout

RATING	DISTANCE	HIKING TIME
★★★☆☆	2.6 miles round-trip	1 hour

ELEVATION GAIN	HIGH POINT	DIFFICULTY
850 feet	1,824 feet	◆◆◇◇◇

BEST SEASON
Jan Feb **Mar** **Apr** May Jun Jul Aug Sep **Oct** **Nov** Dec

The Hike

Restored in 2002 by the Everett Mountaineers, this cabin atop a 70-foot tower affords stunning views across the Skykomish Valley to Mount Index and Bridal Veil Falls and east to the rocky rabbit ears of Mount Baring. Relatively low for a lookout—just over 1,800 feet—it's one of the most easily accessed lookouts in the state. The 89 steps upward lead to a large public observation platform and enclosed cabin, maintained by the Everett Mountaineers.

Getting There

Head east on Highway 2 to milepost 37.6, about 23 miles east of Monroe. The trailhead and roadside parking area are on the left (north) side of Highway 2. Elevation: 850 feet.

PERMITS/CONTACT
None required/Mount Baker–Snoqualmie National Forest, Skykomish Ranger District, (360) 677-2414

MAPS
USGS Index; Green Trails Index 142

TRAIL NOTES
Leashed dogs okay; kid-friendly; great views

Heybrook Lookout affords stunning views over the Skykomish Valley

The Trail

On paper this trail has all the components of an epic Cascadian day-hiking adventure: a dark, forested climb under a canopy so thick the sun can't penetrate despite its best efforts; an emergence from the trees into open space, where views expand and the jaw drops; and, finally, a historic lookout where one can contemplate those who've come before—except that everything's in miniature. The forested

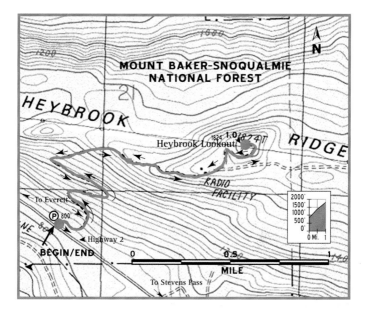

climb is only a mile, and chances are you'll reach the lookout's observation deck in a half-hour from when you slam your car door shut.

From the trailhead climb fairly steadily through dense second growth—the ridge was clear-cut in the 1920s—watching your step, as the trail can be a tad rocky in spots. In about a half-mile take note that more blue sky is poking through the trees. Not long after, views open up to the right, and up and to your left there stands the lookout's six-story tower. Views across the Skykomish Valley are impressive, but head to the observation deck near the top for even more. There, to the east, you'll see Mount Baring's craggy twin summit, fewer than 5 air miles away, and to the west, the sparkling waters of Puget Sound.

The first fire lookout on the site was built in 1932 and rebuilt in the early 1960s, when an extra 20 feet was added to its tower. In the early 1970s the lookout was retired and the structure fell into disrepair. After some nifty renovations by the Everett Mountaineers, however, the tower opened again in 2003. ■

6. Barclay Lake

RATING	DISTANCE	HIKING TIME
★★★☆☆	4.4 miles round-trip	2 hours

ELEVATION GAIN	HIGH POINT	DIFFICULTY
500 feet	2,422 feet	♦◇◇◇◇

BEST SEASON
Jan Feb **Mar Apr May Jun Jul Aug Sep Oct Nov** Dec

The Hike

Perfect for kids, this not-too-long forest walk rolls along a creek, gaining a net 200 vertical feet to a wonderful lakeside retreat at the foot of impressive-as-heck Mount Baring. There's lots of room for exploration, as evidenced by the kids along the way who are experiencing—or just about to—their first overnighter in the woods. This is a popular trail, so visit at the beginning or end of the season, when crowds are smaller.

Getting There

Head east on Highway 2 to milepost 41.2, about 6 miles east of Mount Index. Turn left onto Barclay Creek Road (Forest Road 6024) and follow it for 4.5 miles to the road-end trailhead parking lot. Elevation: 2,200 feet.

The Trail

Paralleling Barclay Creek pretty much the entire way, this gentle wooded path passes through mixed forest, from time to time opening up to reveal rock walls just beyond the canopy. But don't feel like you're missing out on anything: Barclay Lake sits at the foot of Mount Baring and its 6,125 feet of pure granite. In the meantime, enjoy the lush mix of old- and not-so-old-growth trees, deer ferns, trillium, wood violets, bleeding hearts, salmon berries, and more.

   At about **1.0** mile reach the first of several stretches of boardwalk. These are great at keeping you from shoe-sucking mud but can themselves be slippery as heck when wet. Be careful. About a half-mile later cross Barclay Creek via a log bridge and go right, climbing a bit

The bunny ears of Mount Baring

PERMITS/CONTACT
Northwest Forest Pass required/Mount Baker–Snoqualmie National Forest,
Skykomish Ranger District, (360) 677-2414

MAPS
USGS Baring; Green Trails Monte Cristo 143

TRAIL NOTES
Leashed dogs okay; kid-friendly; stunning lake and Mount Baring views

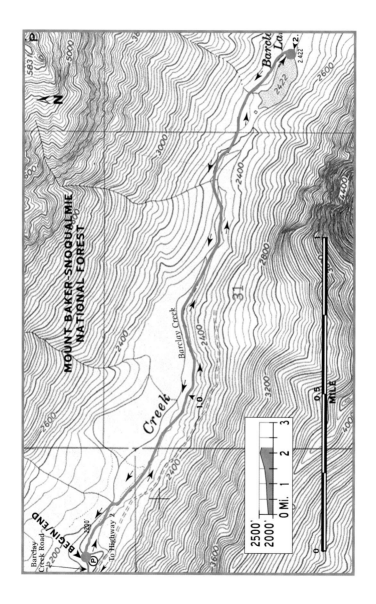

as the trail begins its homestretch for the lake. At **2.0** miles cross a small creeklet—expect a wet foot or two—and look right and up for the stunning straight-on views of Mount Baring. Continue for another quarter-mile to the lake.

From lakeside the granite walls of Mount Baring rise 3,700 feet seemingly straight up and seemingly right out of the water. You'll find yourself scratching your head at some of the tiny rock perches high on the mountain where individual trees are able to grow. Scan the mountain's forested flank for a plunging horsetail of water cascading its way down the mountainside. Skip some stones. Throw in a line. Take a load off. You'll want to stay a while.

Going Farther

For those in the mood for a lung-buster, a primitive trail leads north (opposite of Mount Baring) from the east side of the lake (the far side from where you came) to Eagle Lake, about 1.8 miles farther and 1,500 feet higher. Along with the lake, you'll find wildflower meadows and Alaska cedars more than three hundred years old. Lakeside camping is allowed at Barclay and Eagle Lakes, and at Money Creek Campground just off Highway 2, near milepost 45. ∎

STEVENS PASS/ NASON RIDGE

7. Deception Falls Nature Trail

RATING	DISTANCE	HIKING TIME
★★☆☆☆	0.5-mile loop	30 minutes
ELEVATION GAIN	HIGH POINT	DIFFICULTY
140 feet	1,800 feet	◆◇◇◇◇

BEST SEASON
Jan Feb Mar Apr **May Jun Jul Aug Sep** Oct Nov Dec

The Hike

For a short jaunt this trail packs in a bunch of features—the gravity-meets-water drama that is Deception Falls, some big ole trees, and the opportunity to see the Tye River making a hard right turn when confronted with logs and a giant boulder. Interpretive signs supply the lowdown on what you're seeing.

Getting There

Head east on Highway 2 about 7 miles past Skykomish. The Deception Falls Nature Trail and Picnic Area parking lot is on your left. Elevation: 1,800 feet.

The Trail

Take a moment to read the trailhead kiosk, which takes you on a momentary journey back in time. Near this spot in the middle of the night on January 6, 1893, the last spike was driven, completing the

PERMITS/CONTACT
Northwest Forest Pass required/Mount Baker–Snoqualmie National Forest, Skykomish Ranger District, (360) 677-2414

MAPS
USGS Scenic; Green Trails Stevens Pass 176

TRAIL NOTES
Leashed dogs okay; kid-friendly; 0.2-mile is barrier-free

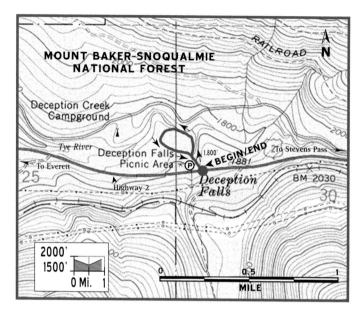

transcontinental Great Northern Railway—1,800 miles of railroad connecting Puget Sound with Saint Paul, Minnesota. Wow.

As for the trail, from behind the kiosk head down and follow the loop trail into a dark, lush forest of cedars, hemlock, and firs. About three hundred years ago a forest fire swept through these parts; the cedars survived, whereas the hemlocks and firs have grown in since then. This natural history tidbit is courtesy one of the many interpretive signs that, along with spiffy viewing platforms, can be found along the trail.

As for the falls, head to the right and follow the rumble. In a couple hundred yards, you'll reach the tumbling falls. Just under Highway 2, Deception Creek squeezes its way through boulders and bedrock plummeting about 60 feet in a thunderous display. It's a tremendous crash and an exciting show. Make sure to hold the hands of young ones.

The rushing waters of Deception Creek

Once sated, resume following the trail loop and gape at the Tye River, which at one point makes a hard, hard right turn, as if at the last moment it remembered someplace it was supposed to flow. All along the water, listen and look for water ouzels, robin-sized birds that feed underwater and sometimes nest behind waterfalls. ■

8. Iron Goat Trail

RATING	DISTANCE	HIKING TIME
★★★★☆	6.0 miles point-to-point	4 hours

ELEVATION GAIN	HIGH POINT	DIFFICULTY
700 feet	3,100 feet	◆◇◇◇◇

BEST SEASON
~~Jan~~ ~~Feb~~ ~~Mar~~ ~~Apr~~ May Jun Jul Aug Sep Oct Nov ~~Dec~~

The Hike

Here's a really great hands- and feet-on lesson about railroad history in the Northwest. Passing several abandoned tunnels and snow sheds, the Iron Goat Trail follows the old Great Northern Railway that crossed Stevens Pass more than one hundred years ago. Interpretive signs along the way fill you in about the whos, whats, wheres, whens, and whys.

Getting There

The trail is a 6.0-mile point-to-point trail from the Martin Creek trailhead at the west end to the Wellington trailhead at the east. To get to the Martin Creek trailhead, where you'll begin, go east on Highway 2 to just past milepost 55, about 6 miles past Skykomish. Turn left onto the Old Cascade Highway, following the sign for Iron Goat Trail. In 2.3 miles turn left on Forest Road 6710 and continue for 1.4 miles to the Martin Creek trailhead parking lot. Elevation: 2,500 feet.

PERMITS/CONTACT
Northwest Forest Pass required/Mount Baker–Snoqualmie National Forest, Skykomish Ranger District, (360) 677-2414

MAPS
USGS Scenic; Green Trails Stevens Pass 176

TRAIL NOTES
Leashed dogs okay; kid-friendly; great views; fascinating piece of railroad history; cool tunnel-like snow sheds

Tunnel entrance to Wellington trailhead

To get to the Wellington trailhead, continue east on Highway 2 to milepost 64.4, just west of Stevens Pass, and turn left on the Old Cascade Highway. (If you're coming from the west, because of limited sight distance it's probably best to proceed to the Stevens Pass area, where visibility is better; turn around there and head back to milepost 64.4 and the Old Cascade Highway.) Continue on the Old Cascade Highway for 2.8 miles to FR 50. Turn right and follow for a few hundred yards to the Wellington trailhead parking lot. Elevation: 3,100 feet.

The Trail

From the trailhead kiosk, head south on a boardwalk trail that soon becomes a wide gravel path. In about 200 yards head left and up,

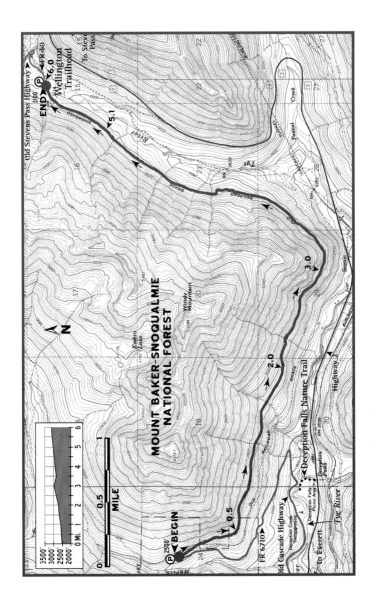

N

MOUNT BAKER-SNOQUALMIE NATIONAL FOREST

Windy Mountain

Embro Lake

Old Stevens Pass Highway

Wellington Trailhead

END

FR 450

6.0

5.1

3.0

2.0

0.5

BEGIN

2500'

FR 6710

Old Cascade Highway

Deception Falls Nature Trail

Deception Falls Picnic Area

Deception Creek Campground

Deception Falls

Tye River

To Everett

Highway 2

Scenic

To Stevens Pass

Tye

3100'

MILE
0.5

0 0.5 1 2 3 4 5 6 Mi.

3500'
3000'
2500'
2000'

following the sign for Martin Creek Crossover. This narrow, rocky stretch climbs for a couple hundred yards but is the trail's steepest ascent. (This being an old railroad grade, the pitch is very gradual—about 2 percent, or around 100 feet per mile.) Just after the trail levels out, take note of the jumble of logs, which are all that remain of snow sheds that were built to hold back snowslides when the railroad was being built. They look like lava flows consisting of wood.

At **0.5** mile pass the first of several abandoned tunnels. Feel free to look, but as the interpretive signs tell you, don't enter. About a mile farther you reach the first of several concrete walls, the remains of a reservoir and spillway from the Great Northern Railway. Lots of water still spills its way over the top, so expect wet feet. Cascade views open up to the right at about **2.0** miles and continue on and off for the rest of the trail. Look down at what appear to be toy cars and eighteen-wheelers on Highway 2. Just ahead, pass another tunnel, taking care to tiptoe along a rocky stretch that follows.

About a half-mile farther cross the narrow top of a spillway wall and follow that with a jumble of boulders. At **3.0** miles the Windy Point Tunnel offers a nice place for picnicking and contemplating the history of this place. In 1910, near the old town site of Wellington, a huge avalanche crashed down Windy Mountain above you, killing nearly a hundred people sitting in train cars that were delayed by heavy snowfall.

Just ahead, for those in need, an open-air privy overlooking Highway 2 offers a true loo with a view. (Ahem.) About three-quarters of a mile ahead, pass the bizarre twisted, molten-looking remains of another shed. At **5.1** miles enter a 0.6-mile snow shed/tunnel that's open to the right. The wide dirt path offers an unusual hiking experience and protection from the elements. Make *chugga-chugga-wooo-wooo!* sounds and pretend you're a train. (I know I do.) At **6.0** miles emerge from the tunnel and arrive at the Wellington trailhead, the other point of this point-to-point hike.

Going Farther
Shorter, barrier-free interpretive trails are located at both trailheads. ■

9. Grace Lakes

RATING	DISTANCE	HIKING TIME
★★☆☆☆	4.0 miles round-trip	3 hours

ELEVATION GAIN	HIGH POINT	DIFFICULTY
900 feet	4,800 feet	◆◆◇◇◇

BEST SEASON
Jan Feb Mar Apr May Jun **Jul Aug Sep Oct** Nov Dec

The Hike

With their promise of wide-open views, ski areas often offer access to some surprisingly worthwhile hiking. Stevens Pass is no exception. Tucked behind the Brooks Chair is this magical land of hidden lakes, heathery meadows, and, when the season is right, blueberries galore.

Getting There

Go east on Highway 2 to Stevens Pass, about 65 miles east of Everett. Turn right into the large Stevens Pass Ski Area parking lot. Because the ski area parking lots just on the west (near) side of the pass are often gated in summer and fall, park in the large lot on the right, just past the Stevens Pass sign. Elevation: 4,060 feet.

PERMITS/CONTACT
Northwest Forest Pass required/Mount Baker–Snoqualmie National Forest, Skykomish Ranger District, (360) 677-2414

MAPS
USGS Stevens Pass (trail not shown); Green Trails Stevens Pass 176 (trail not shown)

TRAIL NOTES
Leashed dogs okay; kid-friendly; great views; peaceful lakes

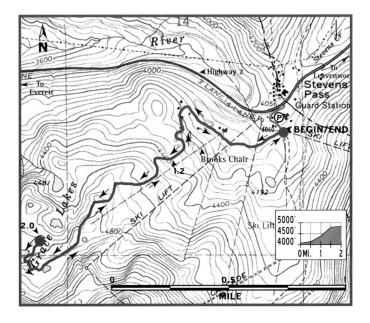

The Trail

Improvisation is the name of the game early on with this trail. From the parking lot, walk through the ski area's main entrance, past the restaurants and lift-ticket booths, and bear to the right (west) past the Skyline Chair to the chairlift at the far west end of the ski area. Follow the dirt access road parallel to the lift. That's your ride up.

Like a ski lift, the road climbs fairly quickly (although not at the rate of a high-speed quad), with views of surrounding peaks opening up. Open ski slopes mean open meadows, which means midsummer wildflower mania. You know the saying: take some time to stop and smell the Indian paintbrush. Views expand the higher you go, and Stevens Pass—where east meets west—shrinks smaller and smaller both in sight and sound. Because much of the trail is in the open, in midsummer it can be hot. Be sure to take plenty of water, especially if there are young ones along.

A peaceful pond above Stevens Pass

The road swings back and forth under the chair, and at about **1.2** miles go straight at an intersection with a road to the right. Reach the top of the Brooks Chair a couple hundred yards ahead. Directly behind it, find the trail that drops down to the first lake, which is mere yards away. If you have young ones who've asked "How much farther?" maybe seven million times today, this first lake makes a suitable picnic or turnaround spot.

If not turning back here, continue on to one of the five fir forest–rimmed Grace Lakes, accessed via various heather-lined exploratory paths that are rarely maintained. The largest is Summit Lake, a curious name for a lake that is the second lowest of them. Keep track of your exploration so you can easily find your way out. ■

10. Bygone Byways Interpretive Trail

RATING	DISTANCE	HIKING TIME
★★★ ☆☆	0.5-mile loop	30 minutes
ELEVATION GAIN	HIGH POINT	DIFFICULTY
None	3,000 feet	◆ ◇ ◇ ◇ ◇

BEST SEASON
Jan Feb Mar Apr May Jun **Jul Aug Sep Oct** Nov Dec

The Hike
Like the Deception Falls and Iron Goat Trails on the west side of Stevens Pass, this short, interpretive loop at the east end of the Stevens Pass Historic District tells the story of the Great Northern Railroad, which first crossed the Cascades in 1893. Great stuff for history buffs.

Getting There
This trail can only be accessed from the westbound lanes of Highway 2, so if you're coming from the west, drive to milepost 71 just past the Stevens Pass Nordic Center. Turn left and left again onto the westbound lanes. The roadside parking area is about a mile ahead on the right. Elevation: 3,000 feet.

PERMITS/CONTACT
None required/Okanogan-Wenatchee National Forest, Wenatchee River Ranger District, (509) 548-2550

MAPS
Trailhead interpretive sign with map

TRAIL NOTES
Leashed dogs okay; kid-friendly; barrier-free; fun railroad history

Site of the Great Northern Railway's former "Tote Road"

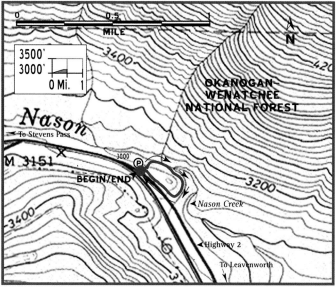

The Trail

As the trailhead interpretive sign informs, this trail passes through four slices of history. In the late nineteenth century, it was the route on which draft horses pulled supplies up the mountain to waiting construction crews who were, as the song goes, workin' on the railroad. They called it the "Tote Road." Then it became part of the Great Northern Railway, used until the late 1920s, when a second tunnel was built. Next the first automobiles struggled up to the pass on one of the first roads across the Cascades. And today, well, Highway 2 passes through here, mere yards from the old Tote Road.

The easy-to-follow path meanders through pleasant forest, some craggy outcrops, and alongside Nason Creek, which impresses with mini waterfalls. Various artifacts (such as an old oven) hearken to the area's past; pick up a brochure at the trailhead so you know what you're seeing. ■

11. Rock Mountain

RATING	DISTANCE	HIKING TIME
★★★★☆	11.0 miles round-trip	6 hours
ELEVATION GAIN	**HIGH POINT**	**DIFFICULTY**
4,100 feet	6,850 feet	◆◆◆◆◆
	BEST SEASON	
	Jan Feb Mar Apr May **Jun Jul Aug Sep Oct** Nov Dec	

The Hike

Don't believe whatever bad things you've read about this trail—if you're an alpine vista hound, Rock Mountain seriously rocks! Sure, it's steep—more than 4,000 feet vertical in about 5.5 miles—and there's no water on the climb, or shade either, but that just means you have views almost the entire way. Take lots to drink, spread the sunscreen, wear a hat, and you'll be fine.

Getting There

Go east on Highway 2 to milepost 73.1, about 8 miles past Stevens Pass. The signed trailhead is just off the highway, north up a short dirt road. Elevation: 2,800 feet.

The Trail

I'm not a personal crusade kind of guy, but when it comes to this trail, I'll crusade. One of the higher points along Nason Ridge, just east of Stevens Pass, the Rock Mountain Trail is a great hike that for whatever reason has gotten bad press in the guidebooks. They slam Rock Mountain for being too steep with relentless switchbacks, which, okay, might be kind of true. But, hello, this *is* hiking we're talking about here, not mall walking.

Besides, the 360-degree alpine views from the top are stupendous—everything from nearby Mount Howard to Glacier Peak to dry-side Lake Wenatchee, Icicle Ridge, and the Stuart Range gang. Turn your head a skosh and there are the dark forests and river valleys of rain-soaked Western Washington. Also, huge in my book, the trailhead is right off Highway 2, meaning no winding, scary, potholed road that rattles your fillings and makes your toupee flip-flop off your head. Nowhere else on Highway 2 or Interstate 90 can you pull off the road and in fewer than five minutes be hiking a trail that tops out at nearly 7,000 feet. And, because this is south-facing, you can get quite high (elevation-wise) quite early in the season.

There. I feel better.

PERMITS/CONTACT
Northwest Forest Pass required/Okanogan-Wenatchee National Forest, Wenatchee River Ranger District, (509) 548-2550

MAPS
USGS Mount Howard; Green Trails Wenatchee Lake 145

TRAIL NOTES
Leashed dogs okay; great mountain views; quite steep

Mount Howard, in the near distance, appears just a stone's throw from Rock Mountain

Now, from the trailhead, cross under some high-tension wires via an old road and begin climbing. Head up, way up, by tiny little switchbacks that make you feel like a duck in a shooting gallery. First you're facing east, thirty seconds later you're facing west, then you're facing east, then west, then east, then west. But you're in the open, which can be a bane if it's hot out, but it is more often a boon because the views keep improving with every step, giving you a sense of the progress you're making. After about **3.5** miles, just over 5,500 feet,

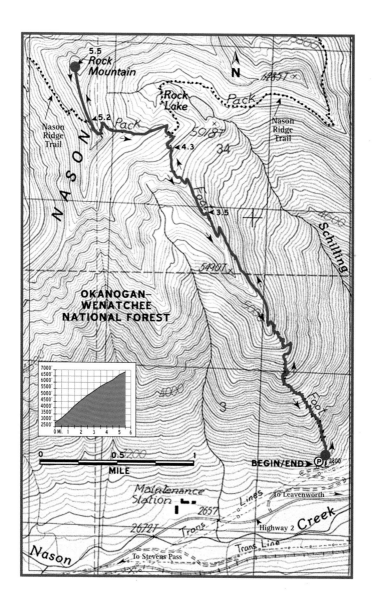

5.5 *Rock Mountain*

Rock Lake

Pack

18851 ×

N

Nason Ridge Trail

Nason Ridge Trail

5.2 Pack

59187

4.3

34

Pack

3.5

4600

Schilling

54981 ×

OKANOGAN–WENATCHEE NATIONAL FOREST

7000'
6500'
6000'
5500'
5000'
4500'
4000'
3500'
3000'
2500'
0 Mi. 1 2 3 4 5 6

4000'

3

Rock

0   0.5   5200   1

MILE

BEGIN/END ▶ Ⓟ 2800

Maintenance Station

2657

2672T

Trans

Trans Line

Lines

To Leavenworth

Highway 2 **Creek**

Nason

To Stevens Pass

reach a slightly alarming area with warning signs reading "Danger Artillery Area." In winters they blast here for avalanches, and further signs caution that if you see an unexploded shell, stay away. Will do.

Nason Ridge, about 700 feet above, beckons, as do wildflowers that fill this meadowy mountainside. Climb steadily to **4.3** miles and the ridgetop intersection with the Nason Ridge Trail, which stretches for about 20 miles from near Stevens Pass to near Lake Wenatchee. Views are big of mountains above, beyond, and below, as well as down to Rock Lake in a basin a stone's throw away.

Go left (west) and follow the ridgeline trail as it climbs about 700 feet over the next mile or so. At **5.2** miles go straight at a signed intersection with the Snowy Creek Trail, and reach the summit in a few hundred yards, at **5.5** miles. Bask in the views and check out the rusty nails and other detritus, remnants of a fire lookout that once occupied this rarified air.

Going Farther

Camping is available at White Pine Campground, about 3 miles east of Forest Road 657 on Highway 2. ■

12. Merritt Lake

RATING	DISTANCE	HIKING TIME
★★★★☆	6.0 miles round-trip	4 hours

ELEVATION GAIN	HIGH POINT	DIFFICULTY
2,100 feet	5,003 feet	◆◆◆◇◇

BEST SEASON
Jan Feb Mar Apr May **Jun Jul Aug Sep Oct** Nov Dec

The Hike

This Nason Ridge area hike takes in an alpine lake that's a true gem that in fall is ablaze with reflected autumnal colors. Options abound for continuing on to Lost Lake or following the ridge to Alpine Lookout, or, in the other direction, to Rock Mountain. But the lake is a worthy destination in itself and merits attention.

Getting There

Go east on Highway 2 to milepost 76.1 and Forest Road 657, about 11 miles past Stevens Pass. A sign on Highway 2 points the way. Follow it for about 2 miles to the road-end trailhead parking lot. Elevation: 3,100 feet.

The Trail

From the parking lot, crane your neck and take a gander up toward Nason Ridge; if you're here in the fall, you'll see it wears its colors well.

PERMITS/CONTACT
Northwest Forest Pass required/Okanogan-Wenatchee National Forest, Wenatchee River Ranger District, (509) 548-2550

MAPS
USGS Mount Howard; Green Trails Wenatchee Lake 145

TRAIL NOTES
Leashed dogs okay; kid-friendly; great lake and mountain views

Fall foliage is spectacular at Merritt Lake

Give a gaze for Alpine Lookout, which is still in use. On the trail, start by climbing through pine and fir forest, inadvertently kicking some of the biggest pinecones I've ever seen in my life—some seemed practically the size of pineapples. The grade is not killer (that is, it's not Rock Mountain–esque), so if you've got a child who is particularly patient, bring him or her along; the lake itself is a terrific payoff.

Views of the Chiwaukum Mountains across Highway 2 poke through from time to time, as do look-sees across to Nason Ridge. At about **2.0** miles cross a boulder field, and after a short,

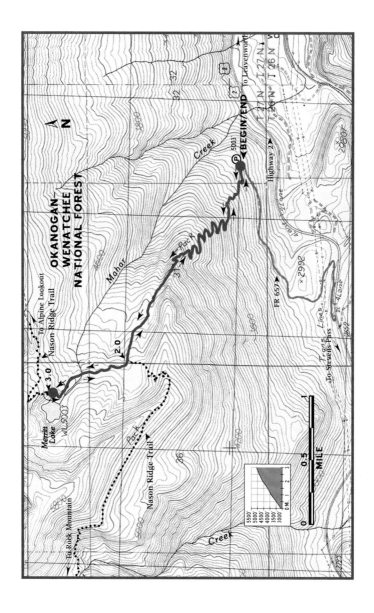

OKANOGAN-
WENATCHEE
NATIONAL FOREST

N

To Alpine Lookout
Nason Ridge Trail

3.0

Merritt
Lake
W 5003

2.0

Nason Ridge Trail

To Rock Mountain

Mahar

Pack

Creek

Creek

BEGIN/END

5003

P

Highway 2

To Leavenworth

T 27 N | T 27 N
T 26 N | T 26 N

2992

FR 657

To Stevens Pass

0.5

MILE

The still-active lookout is often visited by mountain goats

semi-flat stretch, resume climbing consistently. In a few hundred yards reach a signed intersection with the Nason Ridge Trail. Go right for Merritt Lake (and Alpine Lookout, says the sign); a left leads toward Rock Mountain. The next half-mile or so to the lake is relatively flat, through semi-open, if at times damp, forest. In fall the huckleberry plants here don their autumn reds and the effect is quite nice. Reach the tree- and rock-lined lake at **3.0** miles. Lots of open lakeside areas invite exploration and general poking around.

Going Farther

If you're up for more, Lost Lake is a mile past Merritt Lake, but the way is rough, first climbing steeply and then descending more so. Find the trail there along the right (east) side of Merritt Lake. You'll also find another signed intersection with the Nason Ridge Trail, which leads in a little more than 3 miles (one-way) to Alpine Lookout. Much of the way is forested and descends as well as climbs to the lookout.

Camping is available at White Pine Campground, about 3 miles east of FR 657 on Highway 2. ■

13. Round Mountain–Alpine Lookout

RATING	DISTANCE	HIKING TIME
★ ★ ★ ★ ★	10.4 miles round-trip	6 hours

ELEVATION GAIN	HIGH POINT	DIFFICULTY
3,100 feet	6,235 feet	◆ ◆ ◆ ◆ ◇

BEST SEASON
Jan Feb Mar Apr May Jun **Jul Aug Sep Oct** Nov Dec

The Hike

Alpine Lookout might not be the most inspired name I've ever heard, which is a shame because this trail leads to some truly inspiring vistas. Aerial views 3,400 feet above Lake Wenatchee can be had in a mile-and-a-half, and from there it's 3 miles of mostly open ridgetop rambling—check out Mount Stuart and the Enchantment Peaks—culminating with a still-working fire lookout. Your chances of seeing a mountain goat are probably eight out of ten.

Getting There

Go east on Highway 2 to milepost 82.1, about 17 miles east of Stevens Pass. Just past the Nason Creek Rest Area, turn left on really easy-to-miss Forest Road 6910 (Butcher Creek Road). (You'll likely notice

---

PERMITS/CONTACT
Northwest Forest Pass required/Okanogan–Wenatchee National Forest, Wenatchee River Ranger District, (509) 548-2550

MAPS
USGS Lake Wenatchee; Green Trails Wenatchee Lake 145

TRAIL NOTES
Leashed dogs okay; kid-friendly—at lower reaches of trail; great mountain and lake views; historic working lookout; no water on the trail—take plenty

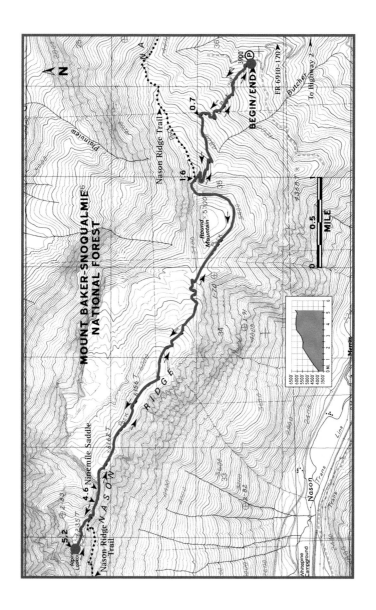

the line of mailboxes before you see the small road sign.) Follow the winding, somewhat-exposed–feeling gravel road for 4.4 miles to a fork. Turn right on FR 6910-170 (this road sign is even smaller and easier to miss) and follow it for 0.2 mile to the road-end trailhead parking lot. Elevation: 3,900 feet.

The Trail

Here's my spiel of debunkery. In all I've read about this trail, it's implied that what keeps this from being a really good hike is the fact that motorcycles are allowed on the ridge. Maybe they are, but I've never seen any evidence of them, such as rutted and worn-out trails. A few years ago when I talked to the ranger living in Alpine Lookout, he said he hadn't seen or heard any motorcycles all summer. So don't skip this trail because you're afraid you're going to run into some X Games competition taking place up on the mountain. You'd be missing out on a gem.

Start by climbing steeply up the Round Mountain Trail through pine and fir forest. At about **0.7** mile enter ghost forest (something you see often on trails on the east side)—silvery snags from fires in the summer of 1994. Most snags are bolt upright, rigidly vertical, but others are curved, side-by-side semicircles that remind you of synchronized swimmers in midroutine. The contrast of these ghostly snags with the abundant ground-level greenery and wildflowers (penstemon, lupine, phlox, Indian paintbrush, and so on) is stunning. Rarely, if ever, is death and destruction so starkly beautiful.

At **1.6** miles reach a signed intersection with the Nason Ridge Trail (Hike 14), which follows this ridge for about 20 miles. Go left and just ahead enjoy views through the trees to Lake Wenatchee and Dirty Face Peak, which looms high above it. For families with small children, a couple of semi-open spots here make for good picnic locations and turnaround points.

Follow as the trail contours around Round Mountain, gaining slight elevation through open forest, and swings south and west along Nason Ridge. From up here, the dark green of the unburned forest looks like cloud shadows. The trail climbs and dips—more climbing than dipping, but most of it is gentle—through meadow and forest along the ridge, affording open views the majority of the time. Mount Cashmere and the Chiwaukum Mountains are prominent in the foreground to the south, with Mount Stuart and the Stuart Range behind them. Below, Highway 2 and Nason Creek snake through the bottom of the valley.

At **4.6** miles drop a couple hundred feet down into a narrow, rocky saddle with semi-exposed feeling drop-offs on either side. This is Ninemile Saddle, but if you're in doubt, look for the tree with the small "9" sign nailed to it. Climbing back out, after about a quarter-mile, reach a signed fork. Go right for Alpine Lookout (left to continue along Nason Ridge; Merritt Lake is about 3 miles west), and after a short, steep climb reach the lookout at **5.2** miles.

Views are all-encompassing—you'll see everything previously mentioned, as well as vistas north toward Glacier Peak and south to Mount Rainier. Note the emerald green waters of the glacier-fed White River in side-by-side contrast to the brownish nonglacial-fed Little Wenatchee River as they pour into Lake Wenatchee. Mountain goats are likely to be seen anywhere and everywhere around the lookout, often with little ones. Take photos, but please do not feed or otherwise disturb the goats.

There's been a lookout here since 1936; the current one was built in 1975. With views to numerous dry ridges and valleys, Alpine Lookout is manned every summer and is a vital cog in Eastern Washington firefighting.

Going Farther

For other Nason Ridge Trails continue 3.0 miles past the Alpine Lookout turnoff for Merritt Lake (Hike 12); Rock Mountain (Hike 11) is about 6.0 miles beyond that. For information on hiking the entire Nason Ridge (Hike 14). Camping is available at White Pine Campground, about 4.5 miles west of the Highway 2/FR 6910 intersection. ■

14. Nason Ridge

RATING	DISTANCE	HIKING TIME
★★★★★	Varies, many options, up to 20 miles	Varies

ELEVATION GAIN	HIGH POINT	DIFFICULTY
Varies	6,852 feet	◆◆◆◆◇

BEST SEASON
Jan Feb Mar Apr May Jun **Jul Aug Sep Oct** Nov Dec

The Hike

From near Stevens Pass almost all the way to Lake Wenatchee, the Nason Ridge Trail follows said ridge for almost 20 miles. Much of this mostly meadowed and open forested trail is between 5,000 and 6,000 feet high and features views to seemingly every peak, ridge, valley, and river in the state. Several trails access Nason Ridge from Highway 2 and nearby forest roads, offering options for interesting point-to-point (read: car shuttle) excursions.

Getting There

Here are four access points to the Nason Ridge Trail, starting with Snowy Creek trailhead at the west end to Round Mountain trailhead at the east end. More information for each trail except for Snowy

---

PERMITS/CONTACT
Northwest Forest Pass required/Okanogan-Wenatchee National Forest, Wenatchee River Ranger District, (509) 548-2550

MAPS
USGS Lake Wenatchee; Green Trails Wenatchee Lake 145

TRAIL NOTES
Leashed dogs okay; kid-friendly—at lower reaches of trail; great mountain and lake views; historic working lookout; no water on the trail—take plenty

---

Check out Rock Mountain, one of Nason Ridge's high points

Creek is detailed elsewhere in this guide in its own trail description: Rock Mountain (Hike 11), Merritt Lake (Hike 12), and Round Mountain–Alpine Lookout (Hike 13). For access to these, head east on Highway 2 over Stevens Pass and continue as follows:

For the Snowy Creek trailhead, turn left on Forest Road 6700 (Smith Brook Road) at milepost 68.7 about 4 miles east of Stevens Pass, and follow it for about 5 miles to a sharp switchback. Go straight onto FR 6705 and follow it for 3.5 miles to the Smith Creek trailhead, right by the creek. Note that sections of FR 6705 can be rough. Elevation: 3,500 feet.

For the Rock Mountain trailhead, turn left at milepost 73.1 at the Rock Mountain trailhead sign, about 8.0 miles past Stevens Pass. The signed trailhead is just ahead. Elevation: 2,800 feet.

For the Merritt Lake trailhead, turn left at milepost 76.1 onto FR 657, about 11 miles past Stevens Pass. (A sign on Highway 2 points the way.) Follow it for 1.6 miles to the road-end trailhead parking lot. Elevation: 3,100 feet.

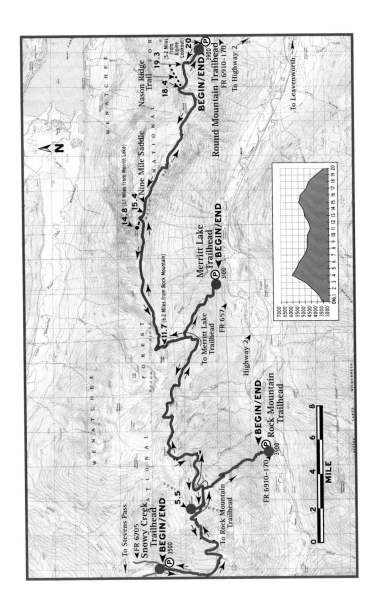

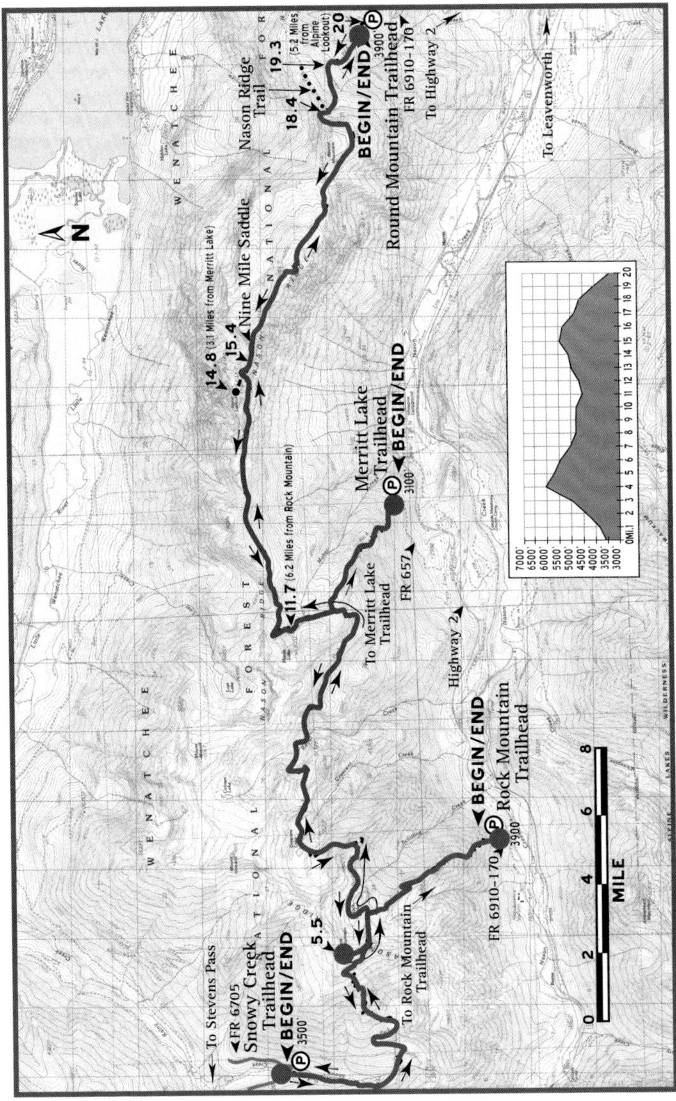
BEGIN/END
Snowy Creek Trailhead
3500'
FR 6705
To Stevens Pass
To Rock Mountain Trailhead
5.5
BEGIN/END
Rock Mountain Trailhead
3900'
FR 6910-170
To Merritt Lake Trailhead
11.7 (6.2 Miles from Rock Mountain)
Highway 2
FR 657
BEGIN/END
Merritt Lake Trailhead
3100'
14.8 (3.1 Miles from Merritt Lake)
15.4
Nine Mile Saddle
Nason Ridge Trail
18.4
19.3
(5.2 Miles from Alpine Lookout)
20
BEGIN/END
Round Mountain Trailhead
3900'
FR 6910-170
To Highway 2
To Leavenworth
WENATCHEE NATIONAL FOREST
NASON RIDGE
N
MILE
0
2
4
6
8
7000'
6500'
6000'
5500'
5000'
4500'
4000'
3500'
3000'
0MI.1 2 3 4 5 6 7 8 9 10 11 12 13 14 15 16 17 18 19 20

For the Round Mountain trailhead, turn left at milepost 82.1 on to easy-to-miss FR 6910, about 17 miles east of Stevens Pass. Just past the Nason Creek Rest Area, turn left onto Forest Road 6910 (Butcher Creek Road). (You'll likely notice the line of mailboxes before you see the small road sign.) Follow the winding, somewhat-exposed-feeling gravel road for 4.4 miles to a fork. Turn right on FR 6910-170 (this road sign is even smaller than the previous one and easier to miss) and follow it for 0.2 mile to the road-end trailhead parking lot. Elevation: 3,900 feet.

The Trail

From the above access points, the Nason Ridge Trail can be hiked for any distance (just turn around when you've had enough), or use a car shuttle for point-to-point hiking. Here's what to expect along the way, going from west to east.

Snowy Creek to Rock Mountain (5.5 miles). Roads gobble up some of the elevation gain you'd otherwise be hiking via the Rock Mountain Trail—this trail starts about 700 feet higher than that trail—but you've still got some climbing to do . . . as in 2,300 feet during the last 3.3 miles to the ridge. Luckily, much of it is forested—the trail begins in old growth—and Snowy Creek offers thirst-quenching hydration opportunities (also known as drinking) on the first half of this trail. The south-facing, minimally forested Rock Mountain Trail can be hot and very dry. Near the top, views and open meadows stretch to infinity.

Rock Mountain to Merritt Lake (6.2 miles). After some glorious alpine rambling with a couple side trips to Rock Mountain's former lookout site and Rock Lake, the trail drops from about 6,000 feet to 4,800 feet in the forest in a hurry, as if it stole something and is making a getaway. There is water, however, in the form of a creek or two and Crescent Lake. Parts of this section can be overgrown, and because in a 2.0-mile stretch near the end it climbs back up to 5,600 feet only to drop back down to 4,800 feet, it has earned roller-coaster designation in my book. The last mile follows the Merritt Lake Trail to the lake.

Merritt Lake to Alpine Lookout (3.1 miles). Climb above the lake to the east and at the signed intersection go right, descending a bit into the woods. Although this stretch isn't nearly the roller-coaster that the previous one is, it does have its mini up-and-down moments, much of it through forest. There's no water to be found on this section. The last 0.8 mile is mostly in subalpine meadow with spectacular views and climbs 600 feet on the way to the working lookout. Watch for mountain goats.

Alpine Lookout to Round Mountain trailhead (5.2 miles). This route consists of more than 3 miles of terrific ridge rambling, with views south to the Stuarts and the Enchantments and north to Dirty Face and Lake Wenatchee. The last 1.6 miles is a downhill cruise through pine and fir forest, including a fascinating stretch of ghost trees.

Going Farther

Camping is available at White Pine Campground, about 3 miles east of FR 657 on Highway 2. ■

LAKE WENATCHEE/
TUMWATER CANYON

15. Penstock Trail

RATING	DISTANCE	HIKING TIME
★★★☆☆	2.4 miles round-trip	2 hours

ELEVATION GAIN	HIGH POINT	DIFFICULTY
130 feet	1,450 feet	♦◇◇◇◇

BEST SEASON											
Jan	Feb	Mar	Apr	May	Jun	Jul	Aug	Sep	Oct	Nov	Dec

The Hike

Also known as the Old Pipeline Trail and the Tumwater Canyon Trail, this mostly level path follows the Wenatchee River on its homestretch to Leavenworth through Tumwater Canyon. There are plenty of spots for lunching, river and rapids gazing, and watching rock climbers spider their way up the sides of Castle Rock. Visit in May and June, when the river is at its most raging.

Getting There

Head east on Highway 2 over Stevens Pass to milepost 97.4, about 32.0 miles past Stevens Pass and about 3.0 miles before Leavenworth. The riverside trailhead parking lot is on the right side of Highway 2, next to a popular swimming beach in summer months. Elevation: 1,400 feet.

The Trail

Like several trails just off Highway 2 (such as Deception Falls, Iron Goat, Bygone Byways), this one's got a bit of railroad history to it. The penstock referred to in the trail's name was a pipeline that once ran through this canyon carrying water to power electricity for the Great Northern Railroad. When the railroad realized that steam engines produced too much exhaust as they powered their way through the Cascade Tunnel on the way to Stevens Pass—everybody on board was getting sick—they switched to electric power; the penstock supplied water to the station producing electric power for the trains.

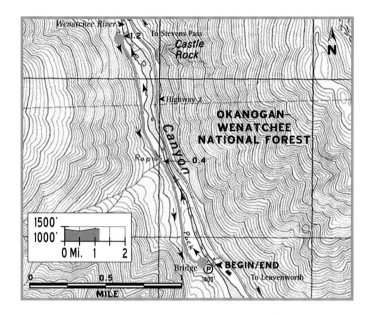

Interestingly, the deck of the bridge you're about to cross is the bottom half of that old pipeline.

From the parking lot, walk a short stretch upstream to a rusty metal structure—known locally as "the Red Bridge"—spanning the Wenatchee River. Oddly, although the bridge itself is metal, the way

PERMITS/CONTACT
None required/Okanogan-Wenatchee National Forest, Wenatchee River Ranger District, (509) 548-2550

MAPS
USGS Leavenworth; Green Trails Leavenworth 178

TRAIL NOTES
Leashed dogs okay; kid-friendly; raging river views

This rusty bridge is an excellent spot for watching the Wenatchee's raging white water

across is a narrow dirt and rock path. Once across, head to the right and follow as the mostly level trail parallels the river for just over a mile.

Chances are you'll stop at many points to admire the river in all its raging, rock- and boulder-bouncing fury, but don't ignore the walls of impressive Tumwater Canyon either, which rise almost a mile above you. Rocky Icicle Ridge on your left is largely adorned with thousands of light-colored snags from past fires, which all blur together making the mountainside look like it had a crew cut that's now growing out. Take note, too, of bits of rusted metal and an old sign from the trail's penstock stage.

At about **0.4** mile cross a creek that, earlier in the year, can be a tad tricky to cross. Be sure to pack your trekking poles. At various points along the trail, little exploratory paths lead to sandy river beaches or flat rocks great for sunbathing. Hold on tight to little ones at points where the river is rushing with enough power to carry them away.

At **1.2** miles you'll find a good turnaround spot, a bouldery area just across the river and Highway 2 from Castle Rock, which you'll know because it rises up out of the hillside for 300 feet and looks . . . like the tower of a castle. It's a popular spot with rock climbers. Peregrine falcons often nest on its ledges, making the climbers find other rocks to scale.

Going Farther

Camping is available at Tumwater Campground on Highway 2, about 7 miles west of the trailhead, and at several campgrounds along Icicle Road, closer to Leavenworth. ∎

16. Dirty Face Peak

RATING	DISTANCE	HIKING TIME
★★★★☆	9.0 miles round-trip	6 hours

ELEVATION GAIN	HIGH POINT	DIFFICULTY
3,900 feet	5,989 feet	◆◆◆◆◇

BEST SEASON
Jan Feb Mar Apr May **Jun Jul Aug Sep Oct** Nov Dec

The Hike

Itchin' to get high (elevation-wise) early in the hiking season? Head for Dirty Face Peak high above Lake Wenatchee. South-facing and dry, you can usually make it to the top of this 5,900-footer by mid-June, sometimes earlier. The expansive views of the Enchantments, Glacier Peak Wilderness, and, of course, down to the lake below are magnificent.

Getting There

Go east on Highway 2 to Coles Corner, about 19 miles east of Stevens Pass. Turn left on Highway 207 and drive for 8.8 miles to the Lake Wenatchee Ranger Station. (Though the building still stands, it is no longer a working ranger station.) Note that the road changes to Lake Wenatchee Highway at 4.6 miles, just past the bridge over the Wenatchee River. The trailhead is just behind the station, about 100 yards up a dirt road. Elevation: 2,000 feet.

PERMITS/CONTACT
Northwest Forest Pass required/Okanogan-Wenatchee National Forest, Wenatchee River Ranger District, (509) 548-2550

MAPS
USGS Lake Wenatchee; Green Trails Wenatchee Lake 145

TRAIL NOTES
Leashed dogs okay; great lake and mountain views; steep; very hot in summer

Clear views of Mount Howard and Nason Ridge from Dirty Face Peak

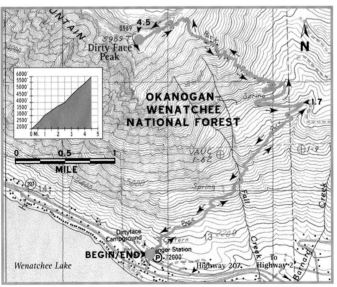

The Trail

Dirty Face gets dirty on you gradually, easing into its whole hard-core elevation-gain vibe while giving you a chance to warm up those quads, calves, and hammys. Arms, too, as lower down the trail can be a tad overgrown and you may find yourself pushing brush out of the way. At about **0.5** mile, Dirty Face starts climbing up this forested, south-facing slope with serious intent. This it will do for much of the remaining 4 miles to the top. Along the way various short trail pullouts offer increasingly spectacular (the higher you climb) views through the trees down to Lake Wenatchee and across to Nason Ridge, as well as providing a chance to catch your breath. A 2005 fire thinned the forest a bit, actually improving the views. Back on the trail, focus on the sunflowers at your feet for a bit to take your mind off the relentless climb. (That only gets worse.)

At about **1.7** miles go left as the trail grants a temporary reprieve and follows an old logging road through the ponderosa forest for about a quarter-mile. The temporarily easier grade disappears, however, where the road bends to the right. In a semi-clearing just ahead, the road turns to trail and—gulp!—this is where the real climbing begins. The trail becomes countless, short little switchbacks intent on leaving sea level in the dust. Over the last 2.2 miles or so, the trail gains about 2,200 feet.

But hey, along the way, you break out of the forest into the subalpine, where spiffy views to surrounding peaks and wildflower meadows at your feet will fairly carry you to the top. (Figuratively speaking, that is.) Reach the top at **4.5** miles. Enjoy views down to Lake Wenatchee, including an interesting marshy area where the White River feeds it. It's the definition of a snaking river. Also check out smaller Fish Lake, and ponder for a moment whether there could be a less inspired name for a lake—Water Lake, maybe? Various peaks and valleys and ridges and rivers extend out seemingly in all directions. Mounts Mastiff and Howard are prominent high points atop Nason Ridge to the southwest.

This spot is the site of a former lookout, and, as such, it is littered with bits of metal as well as the old foundation. They offer some amusement in addition to something to trip over. Watch thine step.

The actual summit of Dirty Face Peak is 2 miles further along the ridge, but it's not easy to get to and, in fact, can be dangerous. But don't feel cheated—it's only 200 feet higher so the burly folk who make it there aren't really seeing much more than you're seeing.

Going Farther

Numerous campgrounds can be found in the Lake Wenatchee area. Three of the closest to the Dirty Face Peak Trail are Lake Wenatchee State Park, Nason Creek Campground, and Glacier View Campground. All are within 12 miles of the trailhead. ∎

17. Hidden Lake

RATING	DISTANCE	HIKING TIME
★★★☆☆	1.5 miles round-trip	1 hour
ELEVATION GAIN	HIGH POINT	DIFFICULTY
230 feet	2,270 feet	◆ ◇ ◇ ◇ ◇

BEST SEASON											
Jan	Feb	Mar	Apr	May	Jun	Jul	Aug	Sep	Oct	Nov	Dec

The Hike

Here's a nice family hike leading to an aptly named lake near the west end of Lake Wenatchee. It's great for lounging about, soaking up the eastside sun, and gazing up at Nason Ridge.

Getting There

Go east on Highway 2 to Coles Corner, about 19 miles east of Stevens Pass. Turn left on Highway 207 and follow it for 3.7 miles to Cedar Brae Road. Turn left and in 0.4 mile go left again following the sign for Cedar Brae Road. In 3.4 miles the road turns to gravel and becomes Forest Road 6607. Just ahead, go left at a fork and at 4.2 miles turn left at the Hidden Lake Trail sign into the trailhead parking lot. Elevation: 2,000 feet.

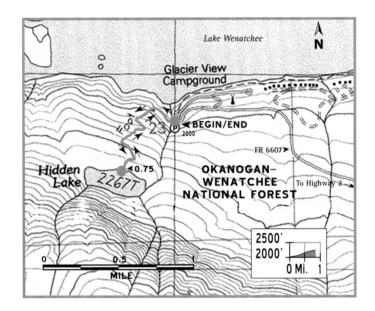

The Trail

This short and not-too-steep trail starts out as a wide, flat gravel pathway. Soon enough it begins climbing through a mixed forest of firs, cedars, and vine maples fanning out across the forest floor. Occasional views of Dirty Face Peak and Lake Wenatchee poke through the trees as the trail switches back and forth across the hillside.

PERMITS/CONTACT
Northwest Forest Pass required/Okanogan-Wenatchee National Forest,
Wenatchee River Ranger District, (509) 548-2550

MAPS
USGS Lake Wenatchee; Green Trails Wenatchee Lake 145

TRAIL NOTES
Leashed dogs okay; kid-friendly

Tucked away at the foot of Nason Ridge, Hidden Lake is all peace and quiet

Keep the young ones occupied by helping them spot woodpeckers that call these trees lunch, and by helping them pick huckleberries in the fall. Luckily the trail is short enough that just about the time you figure you're going to go loony if you hear the question "How much farther?" one more time, at **0.75** mile you've arrived. (When you hear the rushing creek, you can breathe easier because you're just about there.)

The lake itself is a gem. Don't be surprised if a great blue heron flaps its great wings and skedaddles on out of there as soon as you arrive; Hidden Lake is on their places-to-fish list. Nason Ridge rises high in front of you, an impenetrable forest- and rock-wall that keeps this lake hidden. You arrive at basically the middle of the lake's shoreline; trails lead off in either direction, offering the kiddies hours of exploratory entertainment. For those without small children, numerous lakeside boulders in the glorious eastside sun offer the chance for exploring the inside of one's eyelids—that is, snoozing. When it's time, return the same way.

Going Farther

Numerous campgrounds can be found in the Lake Wenatchee area. Three of the closest to the Hidden Lake Trail are Glacier View Campground (located pretty much at the trailhead), Lake Wenatchee State Park, and Nason Creek Campground. All are within about 5 miles of the trailhead. ∎

ICICLE CANYON

18. Icicle Ridge

RATING	DISTANCE	HIKING TIME
★ ★ ★ ☆ ☆	6.0 miles round-trip	3.5 hours

ELEVATION GAIN	HIGH POINT	DIFFICULTY
1,800 feet	3,000 feet	♦ ♦ ◊ ◊ ◊

BEST SEASON											
Jan	Feb	Mar	Apr	May	Jun	Jul	Aug	Sep	Oct	Nov	Dec

The Hike

This picturesque, early-season day hike whets your appetite for upcoming hiking adventures throughout the summer and fall. Although the ridge trail continues for more than 20 miles, you needn't hike nearly that far for superb views of Tumwater and Icicle Canyons, the Wenatchee and Icicle Rivers, and the surrounding mountains. You'll see downtown Leavenworth, too—and feel like you're floating over the city in a hot-air balloon.

Getting There

Head east on Highway 2 over Stevens Pass to Leavenworth, just past milepost 99, about 35 miles past Stevens Pass. Just before entering the town proper, go right on Icicle Road and continue for 1.4 miles to the Icicle Ridge Trail sign. Turn right and follow the road as it bends left, then turn right into the trailhead parking lot. Elevation: 1,200 feet.

The Trail

Start by traversing the hillside through pine forest (some trunks are blackened from past forest fires), climbing gently at first. Soon enough, however, you'll hit your first switchback and the fight with gravity is on. Thankfully, it's a short trail, but this being a southeast-facing slope with nary a creek in the neighborhood, it can be quite hot. (It's made to seem even hotter by the backyard swimming pools and children frolicking therein that you can see in the valley below.) Thus spring and fall are the best times for this approach to the ridge. But with water and sunscreen you'll be fine, even in summer.

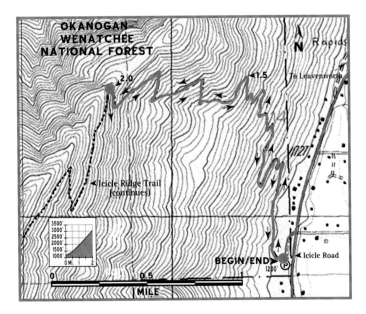

And besides, the many open stretches—largely, the result of forest fires—along the way afford great views down to winding, curving Icicle Creek and its confluence with the Wenatchee River. What you are likely to spot, especially in early spring, are scads of sunflowers—arrowleaf balsamroot—that seem to light up the hillside.

PERMITS/CONTACT
Northwest Forest Pass required/Okanogan-Wenatchee National Forest,
Wenatchee River Ranger District, (509) 548-2550

MAPS
USGS Leavenworth; Green Trails Leavenworth 178

TRAIL NOTES
Leashed dogs okay; kid-friendly; great views

Icicle Ridge reaches for the sky high above Tumwater Canyon

At about **1.0** mile the trail steepens and soon enters unburned forest, but only for a moment. Then it's back in the open and out of the forest for views of the Icicle Valley. The trail climbs steeply over the next 1.5 miles, then hits forest just before the saddle. Reach a shoulder, where the trail temporarily flattens out, at **3.0** miles. As a day hike, this is a great lunching, exploring, and turnaround point. While the trail continues left for another 26.6 miles, go to the right for superb bird's-eye views of downtown Leavenworth and its environs (play a game with your hiking partners where you get points for each pair of lederhosen you spot), and back toward Tumwater Canyon, gouged out over the millennia by the Wenatchee River.

High above, see the rest of the Icicle Ridge, a wall of rock and forest—much of it ghostly white—rising a mile high from river's edge. Take in the raptors digging the thermals up here. Once I inadvertently stumbled on what must've been an eagle-vulture convention. They bolted from the many burned-out snags up here as I approached, but circled and soared high above the town—at what would be eye-level for me—for forty-five minutes or so while I had lunch.

Return the way you came.

Going Farther

From the ridgetop turnaround point, the Icicle Ridge Trail continues for another 26.6 miles, for a total of 29.6. It roughly parallels Icicle Road and can be accessed along the way by such trails as the Fourth of July Creek Trail (Hike 21), about 9.4 miles down Icicle Road, and the Chatter Creek Trail, about 15.5 miles down Icicle Road. Camping is available at several campgrounds on Icicle Road, the closest being Eightmile Campground on Icicle Road, about 7 miles past the Icicle Ridge trailhead. ■

RATING	DISTANCE	HIKING TIME
★★☆☆☆	1-mile loop	1 hour

ELEVATION GAIN	HIGH POINT	DIFFICULTY
None	1,150 feet	◆◇◇◇

BEST SEASON
~~Jan~~ ~~Feb~~ ~~Mar~~ Apr May Jun Jul Aug Sep Oct Nov ~~Dec~~

The Hike

This paved, barrier-free path tells the story of the 1.6 million juvenile chinook salmon that are released each year into Icicle Creek. Visit in late May through July to catch a glimpse of the 1 percent or so who make it back to the hatchery after their 500-mile journey to and from the Pacific Ocean. Interpretive signs along the path and creekside blinds make for plenty of learning and Discovery Channel moments, so this hike is great for families. In winter months, the trails are groomed for Nordic skiing and are quite popular.

The Stuart Range from the Leavenworth National Fish Hatchery

Getting There

Head east on Highway 2 over Stevens Pass to Leavenworth, just past milepost 99, about 35 miles past Stevens Pass. Just before entering the town proper, go right on Icicle Road and continue for about 2.1 miles to Hatchery Road. Turn left and continue straight for 0.2 mile into the hatchery. Elevation: 1,150 feet.

The Trail

This paved loop is a great venue for children and those with disabilities to experience Leavenworth's outdoor wonders. Along with traipsing Icicle Creek's creekside, the trail affords views of the Stuart Range, high atop the walls of Icicle Gorge—all while being able to enjoy a pleasant fish tale along the way. Interpretive brochures available in the visitor center fill in any blanks along this self-guided interpretive tour.

From the parking lot, head past several large holding ponds—home to hatchery fish until they're about sixteen months old and ready to begin their journey to the Pacific—to a bridge spanning the creek. Check out the first of numerous interpretive signs. This one details the differing life cycles of hatchery and wild chinook salmon. At a trailhead just ahead, bear to the left on the paved path. Follow it through meadow and wetlands, taking in interpretive signs pointing out various plant species—scarlet gilia, black hawthorn, ponderosa pine, and more.

At about two hundred yards bear right where going left would be crossing a bridge. (Don't cross the bridge; it's private property on the other side.) Follow the loop around, taking little signed side trips to

PERMITS/CONTACT
None required/Leavenworth National Fish Hatchery, (509) 548-7641

MAPS
USGS Leavenworth; Green Trails Leavenworth 178

TRAIL NOTES
Leashed dogs okay; kid-friendly; barrier-free; spawning salmon in season

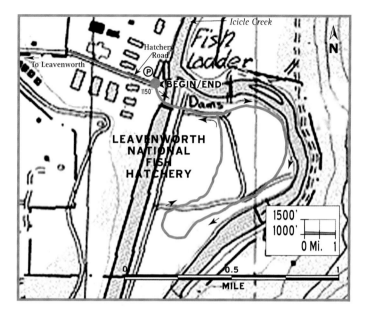

wildlife viewing spots—creekside blinds so the critters can't see you but you can see them—or stopping to take a load off on one of the many pathside benches. Those winged creatures flitting overhead are violet green swallows; in spring they seem to be everywhere. Take your time, enjoy the sights, and return by following the loop back to the first bridge you crossed.

Going Farther

Camping is available at several campgrounds on Icicle Road, including Eightmile Campground located about 6 miles down Icicle Road from the Hatchery Road intersection. ■

20. Snow Lakes Trail

RATING	DISTANCE	HIKING TIME
★★★★☆	13.0 miles round-trip	6 hours

ELEVATION GAIN	HIGH POINT	DIFFICULTY
4,300 feet	5,420 feet	◆◆◆◆

BEST SEASON		
Jan Feb Mar Apr May **Jun Jul Aug Sep Oct** Nov Dec		

The Hike

The Snow Lakes Trail is one of two gateways to the Enchantments, one of the most lusted-after backpacking destinations in the state. But with views of sky-kissing, craggy peaks, icy glaciers, hanging valleys, and tumbling waterfalls, not to mention a couple of crystal-clear alpine lakes, the Snow Lakes Trail is no slouch itself. Plus, as a day hike, there's no need to carry a house-sized pack.

Upper Snow Lake, the gateway to the Enchantments

Getting There

Head east on Highway 2 over Stevens Pass to Leavenworth, just past milepost 99, about 35 miles past Stevens Pass. Just before entering the town proper, go right on Icicle Road and continue for 4.3 miles to the Snow Lakes trailhead on your left. Elevation: 1,300 feet.

The Trail

From the trailhead begin by dropping down and crossing cool, clear Icicle Creek over a footbridge. The rushing stream below will remind you to return to your vehicle if you've forgotten the water. Remember: This is eastside hiking, where in summers you'll swear the sun is twice as strong and twice as close to earth as it is on the west side. Don't forget plenty of water.

Once across the creek, begin the switchback up, first through rock garden, then in and out of dry pine forest, then through scorched forest. In 1994 more than three thousand acres here burned in the Rat Creek and Hatchery Creek fires, which closed the trail for a couple seasons. Today, the trail passes through stands of charred, lifeless tree trunks, which look like giant black toothpicks standing at attention. Take note of the woodpeckers with distinct black backs and necks, which, oddly enough, are actually white-headed woodpeckers. These birds sometimes seem to be pecking away at every snag you pass.

At **2.0** miles a side trail to the right leads to a cool, shady spot, where Snow Creek pools and gurgles. Watch for dippers, those nervous, sparrow-sized birds that can't keep still, and that dive into the creek for

PERMITS/CONTACT
Northwest Forest Pass required/Okanogan-Wenatchee National Forest, Wenatchee River Ranger District, (509) 548-2550

MAPS
USGS Blewett, Leavenworth; Green Trails The Enchantments 209S

TRAIL NOTES
No dogs allowed; great mountain and lake views

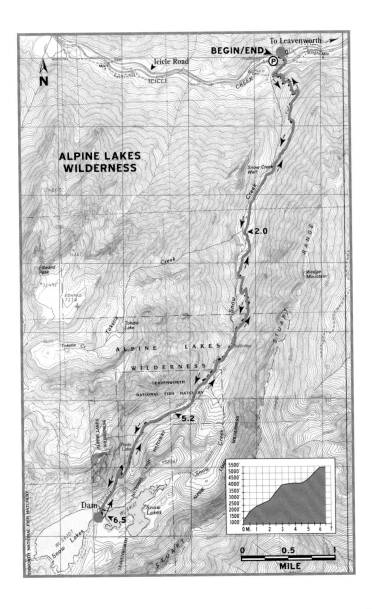

bugs and other grub. A plunging waterfall provides a wonderful back-country soundtrack. It's a shady spot that is great for a picnic and, with its cool pools of water, invites contemplation.

Once you're through reflecting, step back from the trees, crane your neck, and check out 700-foot Snow Creek Wall directly above. For a moment you'll swear that the mountain goats in this canyon are blue, yellow, red, and green—and that they wear jewelry. That is, until you realize that the tiny, multicolored forms moving above are rock climbers, and the shiny glints are evidence of the sun catching in their carabiners. The Icicle Creek Canyon is a rock-climbing mecca, and this wall is one of its most sacred spots.

Back on the trail, after a forested level stretch, the path resumes climbing through both thick forest and open, rocky stretches surrounded on three sides by awesome craggy canyon walls more than 6,000 feet high. About **5.2** miles from the trailhead, the sparkling waters of Nada Lake present themselves, inviting you to take a load off, swat some flies, and bask in the mountain air. It's another great picnic spot or a legitimate turnaround point.

If you're itchin' for more, however, follow the trail along the right side of the lake and head up. Snow Lakes is another 1.2 miles and 600 feet of elevation gain, much of it up a moderately tricky boulder field. For stability, trekking poles, or the ability to grow a second pair of legs in a hurry, are a good idea. At **6.5** miles reach the lakes and the isthmus dam that separates the two. The dam was built in the 1930s and diverts water from upper Snow Lake—upper, as in maybe five feet higher than lower Snow Lake—to the Leavenworth National Fish Hatchery. Return the same way.

Going Farther

To reach the lower Enchantments, continue along the east side of upper Snow Lake and climb about 1,400 feet over the next 2.5 miles to Lake Viviane (Hike 25). Camping is available at a number of campgrounds along Icicle Road, the closest being the Eightmile and Bridge Creek campgrounds, about 2 and 3 miles west of the trailhead. ■

21. Fourth of July Creek

RATING	DISTANCE	HIKING TIME
★★★★☆	**10.6 miles round-trip**	**7 hours**

ELEVATION GAIN	HIGH POINT	DIFFICULTY
4,500 feet	**6,800 feet**	◆◆◆◆◆

BEST SEASON
~~Jan~~ ~~Feb~~ ~~Mar~~ **Apr May Jun Jul Aug Sep Oct** ~~Nov~~ ~~Dec~~

The Hike

Admittedly, the Fourth of July Creek Trail is not for everyone. It's long and steep—climbing almost 900 feet per mile for 5 miles—but it's got a lot of upsides. It's south facing, so it melts out early; spectacular views can be had without hiking very far on it; and early in the season it's awash in wildflowers. One more plus—or minus, depending on how you look at it—you may come across a rattlesnake or two.

Getting There

Head east on Highway 2 over Stevens Pass to Leavenworth, just past milepost 99, about 35 miles past Stevens Pass. Just before entering the town proper, go right on Icicle Road and continue for 9.5 miles to a small roadside parking area. Elevation: 2,300 feet.

The Trail

There I was on a sunny July morning, hiking the Fourth of July Creek Trail by myself to Icicle Ridge, where I was sure to be rewarded with incredible views of Mount Stuart and its Stuart Range siblings, as well as Mount Cashmere and all its homeys—not to mention views deep down into the Icicle Valley on one side and into Tumwater Canyon on the other. I even fancied views to far across the Columbia River! It was a glorious morning. Balsamroot and syringa shrubs brightened the lower reaches of this semi-open pine and fir forest, and even in the first mile I'd enjoyed views to Mount Cashmere. Sure, the trail was steep, but so what? It was just good to be alive.

That's when I heard a suspicious rattling sound. Suspicious, because this early in the hike, the words of the trailhead's posted rattlesnake warning were still fresh in my mind. In the past, I'd never seen a cougar or a bear where trailhead signs had warned me to be on the lookout, so why should this be any different? I'm just jumpy, I thought; or rattled, as it were, but not without reason. For there on the trail about 10 feet ahead of me was a greenish-brownish Western rattlesnake coiling and uncoiling itself.

It was then that I heard a ten-year-old girl let out a high-pitched squeal. Then I realized it was me. Truth be told, snakes freak me out—probably doubly so when I'm by myself. So on that day, I turned around and found another hike and vowed to return with a friend (whom I'd make hike in the lead). Take what you may from that story, my gift to you.

This trail is consistent if nothing else. It starts climbing steeply, continues climbing steeply, and, guess what, finishes steeply, too. In season, there are wildflowers down low, brushy sections in the middle, and avalanche lilies near the top. Two other consistencies: chances for great views exist throughout where breaks in the trees allow, and a lack of water is certain. There's a creek at about a quarter-mile along the trail, but that's it.

At **5.3** miles reach Icicle Ridge. Spin around hills-are-alive-with-the-*Sound-of-Music* style and take in the 360-degree panorama. It truly is spectacular. For a little side trip, hike along the ridge to the left (west) for about a quarter-mile to the former site of an old lookout cabin.

PERMITS/CONTACT
None required/Okanogan-Wenatchee National Forest, Wenatchee River Ranger District, (509) 548-2550

MAPS
USGS Cashmere Mountain; Green Trails Chiwaukum Mountains I77

TRAIL NOTES
Leashed dogs okay; spectacular Stuart Range views; bikes and horses okay; watch out for rattlesnakes

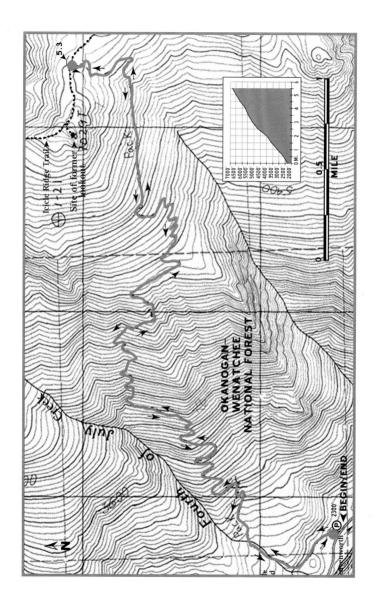

Going Farther

The Icicle Ridge Trail (Hike 18) continues for many miles in both directions, about 29.6 miles in all. It roughly parallels Icicle Road and can be accessed along the way by such trails and trailheads as the Icicle Ridge trailhead, about 8 miles back toward Leavenworth, and the Chatter Creek Trail, about 6 miles west of the Fourth of July Creek trailhead.

Camping is available at a number of campgrounds along Icicle Road, the closest being Bridge Creek Campground, on Forest Road 7601 about 1.5 miles east of the trailhead, and Eightmile Campground, about 2.5 miles east of the trailhead. ∎

22. Lake Stuart

RATING	DISTANCE	HIKING TIME
★ ★ ★ ★ ★	9.0 miles round-trip	6 hours
ELEVATION GAIN	HIGH POINT	DIFFICULTY
1,800 feet	5,100 feet	◆ ◆ ◆ ◇ ◇
BEST SEASON		
Jan Feb Mar Apr May Jun **Jul Aug Sep Oct** Nov Dec		

The Hike

Colchuck or Stuart, Stuart or Colchuck—to which lake should you hike? You can't go wrong with either of these lakes at the foot of the Stuart Range and Enchantment Peaks. Here are some things to consider: both are popular but Stuart is potentially less crowded, given that Colchuck is many backpackers' first stop on their way through the Enchantments. Also, Stuart is 500 feet lower elevation-wise than Colchuck, so there's less climbing involved. Still can't decide? Try eenie meenie miney mo.

Getting There

Head east on Highway 2 over Stevens Pass to Leavenworth, just past milepost 99, about 35 miles past Stevens Pass. Just before entering

Mount Stuart beckons one to the shores of Lake Stuart

PERMITS/CONTACT
Northwest Forest Pass required/Okanogan-Wenatchee National Forest,
Wenatchee River Ranger District, (509) 548-2550

MAPS
USGS Enchantment Lakes; Green Trails The Enchantments 209S,
Chiwaukum Mountains 177, Mount Stuart 209

TRAIL NOTES
No dogs allowed; spectacular lake and mountain views;
horses okay certain times of the year

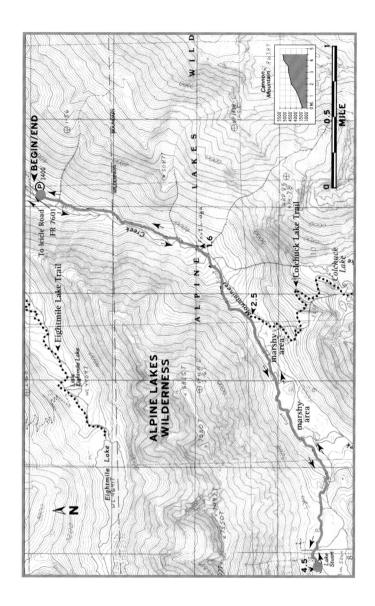

BEGIN/END
3400
P
To Icicle Road
FR 7601
Creek
Eightmile Lake Trail
Little
Eightmile Lake
wl 4041
Eightmile Lake
wl 4641
ALPINE LAKES
WILDERNESS
1.6
2.5
Mountaineer
marshy
area
Colchuck Lake Trail
Colchuck
Lake
marshy
area
4.5
Lake
Stuart
wl 5064

WILD

ALPINE LAKES

Cannon
Mountain 8638†

5500
5000
4500
4000
3500
3000
0 MI. 1 2 3 4 5

0   0.5   1
MILE

N

the town proper, go right on Icicle Road and continue for 8.5 miles to Forest Road 7601. Turn left and follow it for 3.7 miles to the road-end Stuart Lake–Lake Colchuck trailhead parking lot. Elevation: 3,400 feet.

The Trail

After filling out an Alpine Lakes Wilderness Permit, available at no cost right at the trailhead, start by climbing gradually through dense forest. Rushing Mountaineer Creek, which follows you almost all the way to Lake Stuart, and which you eventually cross, provides a soothing soundtrack. Several spots along the way offer creekside access, and occasional breaks in the trees allow for views south to Colchuck and Dragontail Peaks.

At about **1.6** miles cross Mountaineer Creek via a log bridge. (Unless you're of equine nature yourself, ignore the sign for the horse ford.) The grade steepens markedly on the other side, but just ahead, almost as if to apologize, the trail comes to a semi-open rock garden with views to surrounding peaks and ridges.

Return to more steady forest climbing and at **2.5** miles, reach the signed intersection with the Colchuck Lake Trail. Go straight, following the sign for Lake Stuart. Hike downhill for a short stretch and just ahead enter an open meadow with terrific views south toward Mount Stuart. A real surprise is the gentle, almost marshy nature of Mountaineer Creek here, especially given its rushing, rocky nature up to this point. It's almost as if you're on a completely different trail.

Continue south in and out of forest, the marshy creek always by your side. After a final short climb, reach the lake at **4.5** miles. The rocky cliffs of Mount Stuart, the second-highest nonvolcanic peak in the Northwest, rise seemingly straight up, and you're surrounded by geologic wonders on almost all sides—Jack Ridge, the Enchantment Peaks, and numerous Stuart Range all-stars. Follow the trail along the lake to the right for a marshy area where you'll swear you can hear Mount Stuart breathe.

For those of you still wondering whether you made the right choice in visiting Stuart or Colchuck, consider this: the Lake Stuart Trail has better shoreline access. At Colchuck Lake, with its giant lakeside rocky cliffs, getting to the water requires a little work. So dip your toes, take a swim, and float on your back, or close your eyes and relax, confident that you made the right choice. Or if it's early, head back to the Colchuck Lake Trail intersection, head right for about a mile and a half, and decide for yourself.

Going Farther
Keep going up the basin from Stuart Lake for about 2 miles and you'll hit Horseshoe Lake, another high-mountain gem. The Colchuck Lake Trail (Hike 23) uses the same trailhead and follows the same trail as this one for the first 2.5 miles. Camping is available at a number of campgrounds along Icicle Road, the closest being Bridge Creek Campground, on FR 7601 near the intersection with Icicle Road, and Eightmile Campground, about a mile east of the intersection of Icicle Road and FR 7601. ∎

23. Colchuck Lake

RATING	DISTANCE	HIKING TIME
★ ★ ★ ★ ★	8.2 miles round-trip	5 hours
ELEVATION GAIN	**HIGH POINT**	**DIFFICULTY**
2,300 feet	5,600 feet	♦ ♦ ♦ ♦ ◊
BEST SEASON		
Jan Feb Mar Apr May Jun Jul Aug Sep Oct Nov Dec		

The Hike
The reflection of Aasgard Pass, Dragontail Peak, and Colchuck Glacier in the cerulean waters of Colchuck Lake is one of the wonders of the Central Cascades and more than justifies this section of the Alpine Lakes Wilderness being named the Enchantments. This great hike gives a taste of what that alpine wonderland is all about.

Dragontail Peak rises right from the waters of Colchuck Lake

Getting There

Head east on Highway 2 over Stevens Pass to Leavenworth, just past milepost 99, about 35 miles past Stevens Pass. Just before entering the town proper, go right on Icicle Road and continue for 8.5 miles to Forest Road 7601. Turn left and follow it for 3.7 miles to the road-end Stuart Lake–Lake Colchuck trailhead parking lot. Elevation: 3,400 feet.

PERMITS/CONTACT
Northwest Forest Pass required/Okanogan-Wenatchee National Forest, Wenatchee River Ranger District, (509) 548-2550

MAPS
USGS Enchantment Lakes; Green Trails The Enchantments 209S, Chiwaukum Mountains 177, Mount Stuart 209

TRAIL NOTES
No dogs allowed; spectacular lake and mountain views

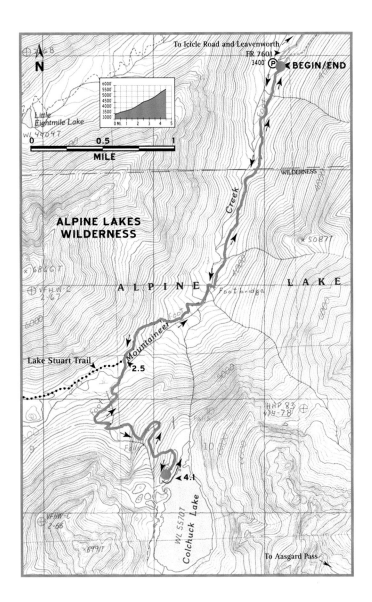

The Trail

After filling out an Alpine Lakes Wilderness permit, available at no cost right there at the trailhead, start by climbing gradually through dense forest. Rushing Mountaineer Creek, which follows you for about the first three miles, and which you cross a couple times, provides a soothing soundtrack. Several spots along the way offer the opportunity to catch your breath while you gaze thoughtfully at the rushing water. (Or not so thoughtfully—it's up to you.) Occasional breaks in the trees allow for views south to peaks you'll be agog over once you reach the lake.

At about **1.6** miles cross Mountaineer Creek via a log bridge. Peer down into the creek for dippers, nervous little birds who seem to think they are salmon as they dive into the water and hop among the rocks. The grade steepens markedly on the other side, but just ahead, almost as if to apologize, the trail comes to a semi-open rock garden with views to surrounding peaks and ridges. Return to more steady forest climbing and at **2.5** miles, reach the signed intersection with the Lake Stuart Trail. Go left, following the sign for Colchuck Lake. (For you nitpickers out there, this is actually the start of the Colchuck Lake Trail; until this point you'd been hiking the Lake Stuart Trail.)

Cross Mountaineer Creek again via a couple of really cool wood bridges and enter a giant boulder field. The way might be a little hard to follow, but bear to the right, staying close to the creek, and you'll soon enough find yourself back on the obvious trail. Back in the forest the trail—a bit more primitive now as it is rocky and root-riddled—climbs ever more steeply, switchbacking up the hillside. Two waterfalls give you an excuse to take a break.

Continuing on, more excuses to pause arrive in the form of giant granite outcrops that offer stunning views to everything from Dragontail Peak to Mount Stuart, Cashmere Mountain, and the entire Mountaineer Creek valley. But stop dawdling: really great views are to be had just ahead. No, not at the next granite outcrop (which is just a few hundred yards ahead) but at Colchuck Lake itself, attained at **4.5** miles after a final short, steep stretch.

Dragontail Peak dominates here, its mirror image reflected in the otherworldly turquoise waters of Colchuck Lake. The somewhat flat part just to the left of Dragontail is Aasgard Pass, one of two gateways to the Enchantments (Hike 25), a plateau of high alpine lakes and majestic rock spires. Lakeshore exploratory trails lead off in both directions, but the one to the left is very short. Those who climb to Aasgard Pass follow the lake around to the right.

Going Farther

The Lake Stuart Trail (Hike 22) uses the same trailhead and follows the same trail as this one for the first 2.5 miles. Camping is available at a number of campgrounds along Icicle Road, the closest being Bridge Creek Campground, on FR 7601 near the intersection with Icicle Road, and Eightmile Campground, about a mile east of the intersection of Icicle Road and FR 7601. ∎

24. Little Annapurna

RATING	DISTANCE	HIKING TIME
★★★★★	15.0 miles round-trip	10 hours
ELEVATION GAIN	HIGH POINT	DIFFICULTY
5,200 feet	8,440 feet	◆◆◆◆◆
BEST SEASON		
Jan Feb Mar Apr May Jun **Jul Aug Sep Oct** Nov Dec		

The Hike

All right, let's say you don't want to do a car shuttle, but you still want to see the spectacular Enchantment Lakes, and while you're at it, climb a nontechnical, mid-8,000-foot peak. Then this is the hike for you. Volcano views abound, from Rainier to Glacier to Baker, and, of course, at your feet you'll spy lake upon tarn upon pond. But first there's that Aasgard Pass thing—2,200 feet of elevation gain in about a mile. Train for this one.

Little Annapurna, a long day's hike in the Enchantments

Getting There

Head east on Highway 2 over Stevens Pass to Leavenworth, just past milepost 99, about 35 miles past Stevens Pass. Just before entering the town proper, go right on Icicle Road and continue for 8.5 miles to Forest Road 7601. Turn left and follow it for 3.7 miles to the road-end Stuart Lake–Lake Colchuck trailhead parking lot. Elevation: 3,400 feet.

PERMITS/CONTACT
Northwest Forest Pass required/Okanogan-Wenatchee National Forest, Wenatchee River Ranger District, (509) 548-2550

MAPS
USGS Enchantment Lakes; Green Trails The Enchantments 209S

TRAIL NOTES
No dogs; spectacular high lakes and mountain views; steep climb up Aasgard Pass

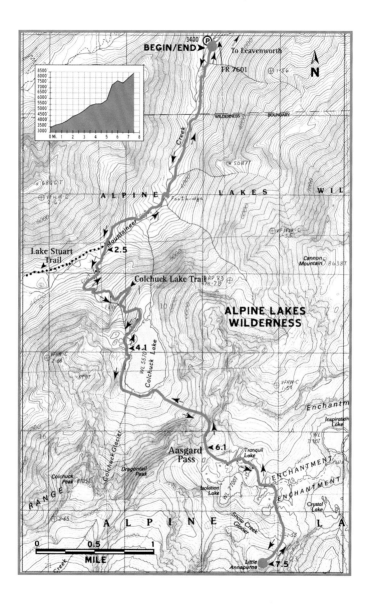

The Trail

Start by following the Lake Stuart Trail for 2.5 forested, Mountaineer Creek–hugging miles (Hike 22). At the signed intersection, go left following the sign for Colchuck Lake, climbing steadily as you do. At **4.1** miles reach the lake and after ample oohing and aahing at the image of massive Dragontail Peak reflecting in the turquoise waters, take note of the notch just to the left that's not all that much lower than Dragontail. That's 7,800-foot Aasgard Pass, gateway to the upper Enchantment Lakes basin. Your first mission, should you choose to accept it, is to make it to the top of that.

Follow the shoreline trail along the right side of the lake until you reach the foot of Aasgard Pass. Sprout wings and fly to the top, or more likely begin the long, hard slog to the top. The "trail," as it were, is mostly a wide gully choked with granite boulders. Caution is key. There's some boot trail, but mostly it's a matter of following strategically placed rock cairns. About a third of the way up, veer to the left just below a cliff band, and about two-thirds of the way up, swing to the right near the top of a gushing creek. Cross one braid of the creek but not the second. Reach the top at **6.1** miles.

Catch your breath and ogle this otherworldly land of lakes, boulders, plateaus, and peaks. Follow the trail east as it zigs and zags around all of the above. Pass Isolation Lake (the first big lake on the right) and, after following a trail of mini tarns for about a quarter-mile, begin veering to the right up the big slope to the south. That's Little Annapurna, named for its resemblance to the 8,000-meter peak in the Himalayas. Of course, from this close it doesn't quite have the same frozen wave appearance it does from a distance, so just be sure to climb the bigger hill to the left.

There's no one single trail to the top, just a mix of boot track and boulders, but for the most part stay to the left. At **7.5** miles reach the top. Views are huge and far-ranging in all directions. Ingalls Creek winds its way down in the valley 5,000 feet below. On clear days, views range from the South Cascades (Mounts Rainier and Adams) to the North Cascades (Mount Baker) and seemingly everything in between. Mount Stuart is just four air miles away and looks almost close enough to touch. To the north, the Enchantment Lakes basin is spread out before you—a true lakes-peaks-waterfalls feast for the eyes.

Return the same way, taking great care on the way down Aasgard Pass, not only for your own safety, but for that of others below. Try not to kick loose rocks down on them.

Going Farther
Camping is available at a number of campgrounds along Icicle Road, the closest being Bridge Creek campground, on FR 7601 near the intersection with Icicle Road, and Eightmile Campground, about a mile east of the intersection of Icicle Road and FR 7601. ■

25. The Enchantments

RATING ★★★★★	DISTANCE 18.0 miles point-to-point	HIKING TIME 12 hours
ELEVATION GAIN 5,000 feet; also loses about 7,000 feet	HIGH POINT 7,800 feet	DIFFICULTY ♦♦♦♦♦
BEST SEASON		
Jan Feb Mar Apr May Jun **Jul Aug Sep Oct** Nov Dec		

The Hike
You've seen the amazing pictures and lusted after it for as long as you can remember. But you've heard how impossible it is to get an overnight wilderness permit to backpack there. The solution? Do the Enchantments as a day hike. Sure, it's burly. But it's one that you'll remember for the rest of your life.

Getting There
This trail description is for a point-to-point traverse of the Enchantments starting at the Lake Stuart trailhead and finishing at the Snow

Lakes trailhead. For the Snow Lakes Trail, go east on Highway 2 to just past milepost 99. Just before entering the town, go right on Icicle Road and continue for 4.3 miles to the Snow Lakes trailhead on your left. Park the finish car here. Elevation: 1,300 feet.

For the Lake Stuart trailhead, follow the Snow Lakes Trail (Hike 20) directions, and continue on Icicle Road for 4.2 more miles and turn left on Forest Service Road 7601. Go left and drive 3.7 miles to the road-end trailhead parking lot. Park the start car here. Elevation: 3,400 feet.

The Trail

What's all the fuss? Nothing much really, just the magical 7,000-plus-foot plateau of crystal-clear lakes, gurgling and gushing waterfalls, rocky spires that pierce the clouds, and mountain goats scurrying across broad granite slabs that await those who venture beyond Colchuck Lake on the west and Snow Lakes on the east. So, get crackin'! One more thing: get an early start. Climbing Aasgard Pass with that east-side sun on your head can be brutal.

Start by following the Lake Stuart Trail (Hike 22) for 2.5 forested, Mountaineer Creek–hugging miles. At the signed intersection, go left following the sign for Colchuck Lake, climbing steadily as you do. At **4.1** miles reach the lake and after ample oohing and aahing at the image of massive Dragontail Peak reflecting in the turquoise waters, take note of the notch just to the left that's not all that much lower than Dragontail. That's 7,800-foot Aasgard Pass, gateway to the upper

PERMITS/CONTACT
Northwest Forest Pass required/Okanogan-Wenatchee National Forest,
Wenatchee River Ranger District, (509) 548-2550

MAPS
USGS Enchantment Lakes; Green Trails The Enchantments 209S

TRAIL NOTES
No dogs; spectacular high lakes and mountain views;
steep climb up Aasgard Pass

At 7,000-plus feet, Isolation Lake is one of the highest of the Enchantment Lakes

Enchantment Lakes basin. In Norse mythology, Aasgard corresponds roughly to Greek mythology's Mount Olympus. Here, Aasgard is the doorway to the Enchantments. Reach the pass and the lakes are yours. There's no foyer, but first you have to get there.

Follow the shoreline trail along the right side of the lake until you reach the foot of Aasgard Pass. Ready, set, climb—as in 2,200 feet in less than a mile. The way up to Aasgard Pass is mostly a wide gully choked with granite boulders that make no bones about crunching a person's ankles or knees. Caution is key. There's some boot trail, but mostly it's a matter of following those who've gone before and thankfully left strategically placed cairns for others to follow. About a third of the way up, veer to the left just below a cliff band, and about two-thirds of the way up, swing to the right near the top of a gushing creek. Cross one braid of the creek but not the second. Reach the top at **6.1** miles and take a well-deserved breather. The views are through the roof, and, as a bonus, it's almost all downhill from here.

Across a vast, rocky, mostly treeless plateau, lakes and puddles and tarns and ponds of every shape and size spread out before you. They're contained by granite stacks and spires that rise high above

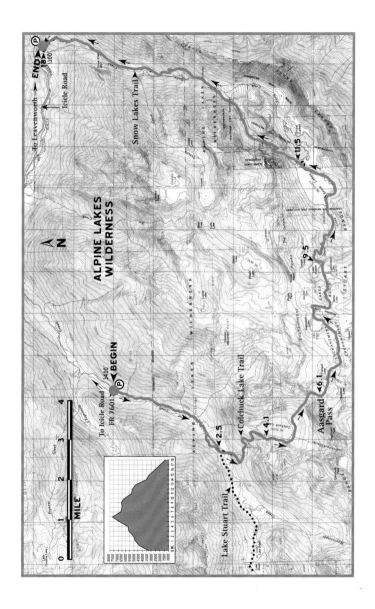

To Leavenworth ←
To Icicle Road
Icicle Road
END ▶
18.1
1300

Snow Lakes Trail ▶

ALPINE LAKES
WILDERNESS

N

ENCHANTMENT LAKES WILDERNESS

11.5

9.5

STUART RANGE

BEGIN ◀
3400
To Icicle Road
FR 7601

MILE
0   1   2   3   4

2.5

Colchuck Lake Trail

4.1

6.1
Aasgard
Pass

ENCHANTMENT

Lake Stuart Trail

on all sides and great rocky slabs that keep the lakes from running into one another. Follow the obvious trail as it zigs and zags past ponds and boulders and rock slabs and waterfalls so numerous that you hear several at once. They all have different tones—gentle gurgle-gurgles, high-pitched swishhhhhes, and baritone swooooshes. If you're using trekking poles, raise one and take a moment to pretend that you're conducting a waterfall orchestra. Take time to explore mini trail spurs that head this way and that.

As this rocky trail of tarns progresses east for about 3 miles, it gradually descends, passing many unnamed tarns and bigger lakes with such names as Isolation, Inspiration, Crystal, Perfection, Sprite, and Leprechaun—all of which are appropriate. I have a friend who says you half expect to see fairies bounding out from behind the rocks here, and it's true. (Fittingly, Bill and Peggy Stark, a Leavenworth couple who began visiting the area in the 1940s, gave many of the lakes such names as Gnome Tarn, Troll Sink, and Naiad Lake, many of which stuck.)

Oft-photographed peaks such as Little Annapurna, the Temple, and Prusik Peak rise overhead. There's more vegetation the lower you go, and the landscape becomes less stark. Asters, Indian paintbrush, and other wildflowers add color to heather meadows, as do the larch forests, which begin changing color usually in September and October.

At about **9.5** miles reach Lake Viviane at the easternmost edge of the Enchantment Lakes basin. Say a fond farewell, vow to be back, and begin dropping elevation quickly on the way down to the Snow Lakes basin. Care must be taken here, for along with being almost all downhill, much of the next few miles to Snow Lakes descends through ankle-crunching boulder fields. At **11.5** miles cross the dam at Snow Lakes and from there, the return past Nada Lake is pretty straightforward. For more detail, see Snow Lakes Trail (Hike 20).

Below the lake, take note of the major gusher shooting out of the mountainside. Tell friends who don't know any better that the lake has sprung a leak and they better act quickly to fix it. (Actually, the upper Snow Lake is drained for part of the year to obtain water for the Leavenworth National Fish Hatchery (Hike 19).) At **18.0** miles shake hands with your hiking partner. You've had a day to remember.

Going Farther

Camping is available at a number of campgrounds along Icicle Road, the closest being Bridge Creek Campground, on FR 7601 near the intersection with Icicle Road, and Eightmile Campground, about a mile east of the intersection of Icicle Road and FR 7601. ■

26. Eightmile Lake

RATING	DISTANCE	HIKING TIME
★★★★☆	6.6 miles round-trip	4 hours

ELEVATION GAIN	HIGH POINT	DIFFICULTY
1,350 feet	4,641 feet	♦♦♦♦♦

BEST SEASON
Jan Feb Mar Apr May **Jun Jul Aug Sep Oct Nov** Dec

The Hike

Although a survivor of both logging and wildfires, this trail to a couple of alpine lakes makes for a fine, not-too-strenuous day hike. Much has grown back since the logging in the 1970s and the fires in the mid-1990s, but this trail, like many in the Icicle Canyon, can be hot and dry, especially later in summer. Seasonal wildflowers provide a pleasant diversion.

PERMITS/CONTACT
Northwest Forest Pass required/Okanogan-Wenatchee National Forest, Wenatchee River Ranger District, (509) 548-2550

MAPS
USGS Cashmere Mountain; Green Trails The Enchantments 209S

TRAIL NOTES
No dogs allowed; horses okay

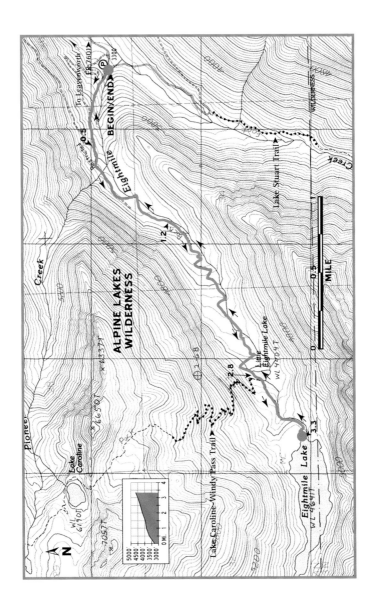

Eightmile Lake, just one of the Icicle Canyon's wonders

Getting There

Head east on Highway 2 over Stevens Pass to Leavenworth, just past milepost 99, about 35 miles past Stevens Pass. Just before entering the town proper, go right on Icicle Road and continue for 8.5 miles to Forest Road 7601. Turn left and follow the road for 3 miles to the Eightmile Lake trailhead. Elevation: 3,300 feet.

The Trail

Start by climbing fairly steeply through open meadow and pine forest. Open means potentially hot (in deep summer) but that's okay. Raging Eightmile Creek accompanies you much of the way, and no one will hold it against you if you foray over to dip your bandana or toes. (Save the latter for the way back.)

At about **0.5** mile, in a dusty open area, the trail joins an old logging road and widens out a bit. The grade immediately lessens, and just ahead the trail crosses Pioneer Creek via a couple logs. (It might be okay to rock hop late in the summer.) At **1.2** miles pass through an eerie stretch of ghost forest, dead tree trunks still standing from forest fires that raged in the Icicle Creek area in 1994. Pass between forest and meadow for the next mile and a half, and at **2.8** miles reach Little Eightmile Lake, which is more a pond than a lake. You'll also reach the signed intersection with the Lake Caroline–Windy Pass Trail (Hike 27).

Water stops in the mountains are always wondrous, but continue on for another half-mile to much larger Eightmile Lake, a favorite of swimmers, anglers, and all-around lake lovers. Its setting is spectacular, ringed by a cadre of rocky peaks, including Eightmile Mountain and Jack Ridge. Also impressive is the massive lakeside landslide of reddish rocks that one might half expect to find on Mars.

Going Farther

The Eightmile Lake Trail shares the same trailhead as the Lake Caroline–Windy Pass Trail. Camping is available at a number of campgrounds along Icicle Road, the closest being Bridge Creek Campground, on FR 7601 near the intersection with Icicle Road, and Eightmile Campground, about a mile east of the intersection of Icicle Road and FR 7601. ∎

27. Lake Caroline–Windy Pass

RATING	DISTANCE	HIKING TIME
★★★★★	15.6 miles round-trip	9 hours
ELEVATION GAIN	HIGH POINT	DIFFICULTY
4,150 feet	7,200 feet	◆◆◆◇

BEST SEASON
Jan Feb Mar Apr May Jun **Jul Aug Sep Oct** Nov Dec

The Hike

This trail doubles your day-hiking pleasure—an alpine lake for the peaceful, easy feeling from the water-contemplation angle, and a spectacular high ridge (almost 7,500 feet) on which you can seemingly roam forever for that 360-degree alpine-view thing. Let it be known that you gotta work—and it's likely to be hot and dry—but while everyone else is heading for the Enchantments just a couple ridges away, you might just have the run of this place.

Getting There

Head east on Highway 2 over Stevens Pass to Leavenworth, just past milepost 99, about 35.0 miles past Stevens Pass. Just before entering the town proper, go right on Icicle Road and continue for 8.5 miles to Forest Road 7601. Turn left and follow the road for 3 miles to the Eightmile Lake trailhead. Elevation: 3,300 feet.

The Trail

Start by following the Eightmile Lake Trail (Hike 26) to Little Eightmile Lake and the signed intersection with the Lake Caroline Trail at **2.8** miles. Go right. The trail begins switchbacking steeply and immediately, as if it stole something from Little Eightmile Lake and needed to scramble up the dry, dusty hillside as quickly as possible.

Pass through the stunning, stark beauty of a ghost forest, dried white and charred black tree trunks that stand bolt upright like massive toothpicks. As on other trails that pass through such stands, expect to be turning yourself around and around trying to spot the

PERMITS/CONTACT
Northwest Forest Pass required/Okanogan-Wenatchee National Forest,
Wenatchee River Ranger District, (509) 548-2550

MAPS
USGS Cashmere Mountain; Green Trails The Enchantment 209S

TRAIL NOTES
No dogs allowed; great views; horses okay

Ghost forest on the way to Lake Caroline

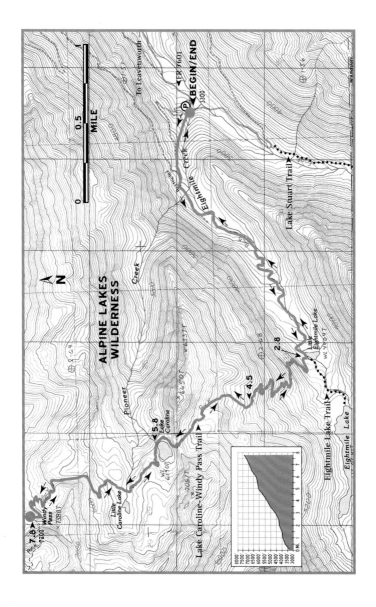

ALPINE LAKES
WILDERNESS

N

BEGIN/END

To Leavenworth

(FR 7601)

P 3300

Eightmile Creek

Lake Stuart Trail

Pioneer Creek

2.8

4.5

Little
Eightmile Lake
wl 4440 T

Eightmile Lake Trail

Eightmile Lake

5.8
Lake
Caroline
wl 6190 T

Lake Caroline–Windy Pass Trail

Little
Caroline Lake

7.8
Windy
Pass
7200

0   0.5   1
MILE

8000
7500
7000
6500
6000
5500
5000
4500
4000
3500
3000

0 MI. 1 2 3 4 5 6 7 8

white-headed woodpeckers that love these trees and seem to be banging their heads on every other one. Presumptuous gray jays are likely to descend upon or near you, thinking that you've come bearing gifts of gorp. The trail itself is often narrow as it cuts back and forth across the hillside, not much more than a sandy ledge really.

Still climbing, at about **4.5** miles, the trail leaves the forest, revealing open views down to the lake and, the higher you go, the Enchantment Peaks and the Stuart Range. Views of Mount Stuart and Little Annapurna steal your focus as you continue climbing steadily through open treeless meadows and glades of larch that come October will take your breath away when they adorn themselves in shades of gold.

At **5.8** miles you will reach Lake Caroline, about 3 miles and 2,000 feet above Little Eightmile Lake. Have some lunch, or go for a dip in the chilly waters. You can turn around and head back now—you've nothing to be ashamed of; it's a worthy destination—or if you can't stop looking at that bare skyline ridge to the north, where you know the views have to be out of this world, get back on the trail and get climbing.

Continue along the east (right) side of the lake. Oddly, the trail takes its time climbing at first—you even drop down into the basin of Little Caroline Lake—but soon enough the trail climbs above the tree line and contours along meadows and bowls that, depending on the month, are ablaze with the colors of wildflowers and fall. Look to the east and see far into Eastern Washington, beyond the Columbia River.

At **7.8** miles reach Windy Pass. You'll know it because its name is well earned, so hold onto your toupee. Views in all directions are wondrous—the Enchantments, the Stuarts, Jack Ridge, and so on. The ridge you're on invites exploration all the way up its spine to Cashmere Mountain some 2 miles away. But watch your time if you decide to explore—it's almost 8 miles back to the trailhead.

An interesting tidbit: At one time, Cashmere Mountain was one of several sites being considered for a $300 million underground space laboratory. The lab would have been 7,000 feet underground and would have conducted research in, among other things, physics, astrophysics, the formation of minerals, hydrology, and microbial life deep underground. The lab would also have studied particles from the sun. Not surprisingly, given Icicle Canyon's reputation as an outdoor recreation mecca, there was strong resistance to the lab.

Going Farther
The Lake Caroline–Windy Pass Trail shares the same trailhead as the Eightmile Lake Trail. Camping is available at a number of campgrounds along Icicle Road, the closest being Bridge Creek Campground, on FR 7601 near the intersection with Icicle Road, and Eightmile Campground, about a mile east of the intersection of Icicle Road and FR 7601. ■

28. Icicle Gorge Trail

RATING	DISTANCE	HIKING TIME
★★☆☆☆	4-mile loop	2 hours
ELEVATION GAIN	**HIGH POINT**	**DIFFICULTY**
120 feet	2,700 feet	◆◇◇◇◇

BEST SEASON											
Jan	Feb	Mar	Apr	May	Jun	Jul	Aug	Sep	Oct	Nov	Dec

The Hike
Pleasant, pleasant, pleasant. That's pretty much all there is to be said about this riverside traipse in the woods. There is almost no elevation gain to speak of, a lot of gurgling, crashing Icicle Creek water to keep the kids interested, and—best yet—it's a loop. (Be still, my beating heart.)

Getting There
Head east on Highway 2 over Stevens Pass to Leavenworth, just past milepost 99, about 35 miles past Stevens Pass. Just before entering the town proper, go right on Icicle Road and continue for about 17.0 miles to the well-signed trailhead on your left, just past Chatter Creek Campground. Elevation: 2,600 feet.

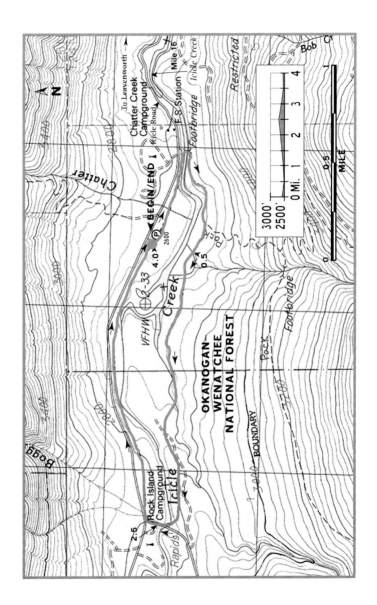

The Trail

As a loop, the trail can be hiked either direction. For our purposes let's take a left and head east (in the direction of Leavenworth). You'll find a map board and interpretive sign, which fill you in on where you're going and what you're likely to see. Start through pleasant pine forest with look-sees and definitely hear-listens of the creek. At about **0.5** mile cross the creek via a footbridge and, now heading west, gain slight elevation as you rise to a nice viewpoint of the river.

Continue west, in and out of trees, taking your time and noticing that the south side of the river is more forested and dark (less sun) while the north side is more open (more sun). Interesting factoid: the Native name for this creek is *Nasikelt*, which according to the legend, sounded to early settlers like "icicle"—hence the name that's attached to seemingly everything in the Leavenworth area. At about **2.5** miles, after crossing a couple creeks pouring down from Jack Ridge, cross back over to the north side of the creek via Icicle Road and pick up the trail on the other side. Follow the creek downstream back to the trailhead, ogling at river views from mini bluffs along the riverbank.

Going Farther

A number of Icicle Road trails can be accessed nearby. Camping is available at Chatter Creek Campground, near the east end of the Icicle Gorge Trail, and at Rock Island Campground, located near the trail's west end. ■

LEAVENWORTH

29. Ski Hill Loop

RATING	DISTANCE	HIKING TIME
★ ★ ★ ☆ ☆	Up to 5.0 miles round-trip	I to 3 hours

ELEVATION GAIN	HIGH POINT	DIFFICULTY
Varies, up to 1,400 feet	2,550 feet	♦ ◆ ◆ ◆ ◆ – ♦ ♦ ♦ ♦

BEST SEASON
Jan Feb Mar Apr May Jun Jul Aug Sep Oct Nov Dec

The Hike

You know how it is for hikers during those spring and late fall times of the year: there's no snow down low but the mountain trails are all but impassible, so where are you supposed to go? Well, the Leavenworth Ski Hill trails offer some fine early season hiking. Gentle loops contrast nicely with a climb up and beyond the ski hill to views of the entire valley. These trails have become popular with mountain bikers, so expect to see lots of two-wheelers from time to time.

Getting There

Go east on Highway 2 to just past milepost 99 and the town of Leavenworth. Once in town, turn left on Ski Hill Drive and drive 1.4 miles to the Leavenworth Ski Hill parking lot. Elevation: 1,430 feet.

The Trail

You're given a couple of choices at the town ski hill. (Doesn't that have just the most nostalgic, small-town, Norman Rockwell–esque sound to it?) From behind the lift ticket booth, a number of tame loops to the east (right) meander through pines, purple lupines, and, when in season, sunflowers, sunflowers, and more sunflowers (including arrowleaf balsamroot). To the west the trail goes up, up, up, and then up some more to a 180-degree viewpoint with big-time views of downtown, Icicle Ridge, Icicle Creek, and the Stuart Range.

For more tame hiking, follow the trail up the hill to the right. Soon you'll hit one or another of several looping road-beds that serve as

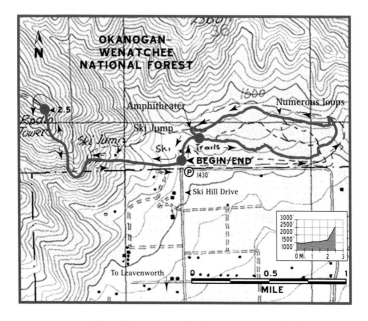

cross-country ski trails in season. It doesn't matter which one you pick—they all seem to head east for a while, then turn back and head west, looping their way gradually up the side of the hill. You're in and out of pine and vine maple forest and may find yourself ducking the occasional dive-bombing hummingbird.

PERMITS/CONTACT
None required/Okanogan-Wenatchee National Forest, Wenatchee River Ranger District, (509) 548-2550

MAPS
USGS Leavenworth; Green Trails Leavenworth 178

TRAIL NOTES
Leashed dogs okay; kid-friendly; great views of town and surrounding area; bikes okay; passes a ski jump and an amphitheater

Top of the highest ski jump in this book

As you continue making sideways loops and figure eights, you'll inevitably find yourself near the Ski Hill Amphitheater. If you want to get up onstage and recite Hamlet's "To be, or not to be" soliloquy to an imagined packed house, I won't tell. (It's not like I haven't done it myself.) Continue until you find yourself at the ticket booth, or if you just want the hills and the views, go left near the entrance gate and follow the obvious trail that climbs straight up toward the wooden structure that'll no doubt have you asking yourself, "People really jump off that?"

The higher you go, the steeper and rougher the trail becomes. At several points you'll probably be using your hands as well as your feet. Reach the top of the ski jump in about a third of a mile, and close to

500 feet of climbing, from the ticket booth. You're rewarded for your hard work, however, with terrific views of the entire Leavenworth Valley and various and sundry peaks in all directions.

For even more above-it-all views, continue in the pine, Eastern Washington–smelling forest for a short stretch to the obvious ridgeline. Bear right through semi-open forest and in about another half-mile—which climbs about 500 feet from the top of the ski jump—reach the base of a communication tower and an open area with spectacular views. (Again, feel free to recite Hamlet's soliloquy.) While admiring the view, one of the first things that strikes you is how many more built-in swimming pools there are in Eastern Washington. On hot days you'll no doubt be scouring your memory banks to figure out if you know anyone who has one and is due for a pop-in visit. ■

30. Blackbird Island– Waterfront Park

RATING	DISTANCE	HIKING TIME
★★☆☆☆	2-mile loop	1 hour
ELEVATION GAIN	HIGH POINT	DIFFICULTY
100 feet	1,100 feet	◆ ◇ ◇ ◇ ◇
BEST SEASON		
Jan Feb **Mar Apr May Jun Jul Aug Sep Oct Nov** Dec		

The Hike

Bird, salmon, history, and river lovers will enjoy this surprisingly secluded trail in what is, after all, a Leavenworth City Park. Much of this loop follows the Wenatchee River. Interpretive signs tell of its rich history as the area's life blood, as well as when to look for spawning salmon (September and October) and what birds call the river home—from eagles and ospreys to widgeons and wood ducks, plus many more.

Summer frolicking in the Wenatchee River

Getting There

Go east on Highway 2 to Leavenworth, just past milepost 99, about 35 miles east of Stevens Pass. Once in town, turn right on Ninth Street and follow it for three blocks, then turn left down the hill into the parking area for Waterfront Park. Elevation: 1,100 feet.

The Trail

This is really a wander-wherever-you-want trail because you can't go wrong whichever way you choose, and all ways lead back to the same place anyway. That said, once in the park, cross the bridge to the right and enter Blackbird Island. The cottonwood-dominant island is the centerpiece of Leavenworth's Waterfront Park and is beloved

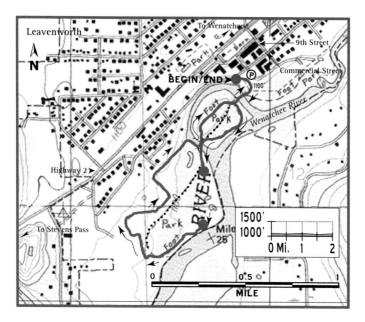

by bird-watchers who scour the island in fall, winter, and spring searching for red-breasted nuthatches, red-eyed vireos, Swainson's thrushes, Bullock's orioles, western tanagers, yellow warblers, cedar waxwings, Calliope hummingbirds, and more.

PERMITS/CONTACT
None required/Leavenworth Parks Department, (509) 548-5275

MAPS
USGS Leavenworth; Green Trails Leavenworth 178

TRAIL NOTES
Leashed dogs okay; kid-friendly; great river views and access; interpretive signs; barrier-free

Trails trace the perimeter of the island as well as bisecting it down the middle, so pick a trail, any trail, and saunter, listening for chirp-chirps of sparrows, warble-warbles of warblers, and bonk-bonks of woodpeckers. Views span east to Icicle Gorge and the wilds of the Stuart Range and Enchantment Peaks.

Along the Wenatchee River are numerous access points, great for taking a dip during those triple-digit summer days or watching eagles and ospreys eye salmon returning in the fall. (You'll see them eyeing each other, too.) Interpretive signs tell the tale of the five-hundred-year flood of 1990, when the river rose so high the bridge you crossed to get to the island was just about submerged. High water submerges parts of the island nearly every spring, depositing logs from upstream.

Continuing west, cross another bridge onto Enchantment Park, which is more of the same, only more secluded. Various exploratory paths head off into the woods and around an artificial pond. Continue west until you reach the golf course, then find another loop home. Or turn around and head back the way you came. You can't go wrong. In winter when snow is present, Waterfront Park makes for some fun snowshoeing and cross-country skiing. ■

31. Peshastin Pinnacles

RATING	DISTANCE	HIKING TIME
★★★☆☆	1.5 miles round-trip	I hour

ELEVATION GAIN	HIGH POINT	DIFFICULTY
470 feet	1,450 feet	◆◆◇◇◇

BEST SEASON
Jan Feb Mar **Apr May Jun Jul Aug Sep Oct** Nov Dec

The Hike
Best known as a rock-climbing destination spot, this desert state park offers about a mile-and-a-half of hiking trails that wind in and out of some of the state's most bizarre rock formations. If you're a climber yourself, "Climb on!" If not, those folks in the funny shoes hanging by ropes and carabiners make for some great entertainment.

Getting There
Go east on Highway 2 to milepost 108.8, about 9 miles east of Leavenworth. Turn left on North Dryden Road and follow it for 0.5 mile to Peshastin Pinnacles State Park on the right. Elevation: 1,010 feet.

The Trail
From the parking lot, pass through a gate and find yourself at the foot of a hillside of numerous sandstone slabs and spires, many that reach 200 feet into the sky. Several look like badly eroded faces that

---

PERMITS/CONTACT
Discover Pass required/Confluence State Park (but they take calls for Peshastin Pinnacles), (509) 884-8702

MAPS
USGS Peshastin; Green Trails Leavenworth 178

TRAIL NOTES
Leashed dogs okay; great river views; amazing sandstone sculptures

---

Eroded rock faces at Peshastin Pinnacles State Park

didn't quite make the cut at Mount Rushmore, or worn-down headstones at some cemetery for giants. Others look like battleships or dinosaurs. Because this is a popular place with rock climbers, many of the formations have names, including Dinosaur Tower, Sunset Slab, Vulture Slab, and Grand Central Tower, among others.

Trails zig and zag up the hillside and loop around a number of the larger pinnacles. It doesn't matter where you start your exploration, as the trails all connect eventually somewhere up the hillside. The higher you go, the better the views south toward farmland, the Wenatchee River valley, and assorted forested ridges, including the spectacular Stuart Range. The only bummer about the park and the trails are the power lines that cross overhead near the bottom of the hillside. But I quibble: just follow the trails up the hill and you won't even notice them. Because this is a popular climbing area, expect there to be ropes and other gear around. Be careful not to step on or trip over it. The hillside can be quite steep and slippery, so take care as you walk up—you may need to use your hands for some scrambling moves in some cases.

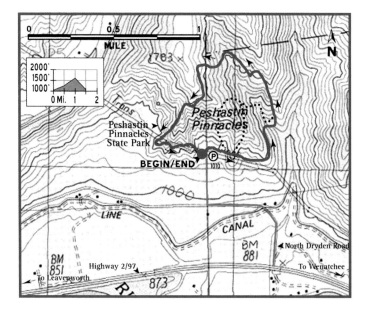

Peshastin Pinnacles State Park boasts an interesting history. Since the 1940s, when it was still private property, the rocky spires have been a rock-climbing hot spot. In the mid-1980s, however, the area was closed to the public because of the owners' liability concerns. In a happy conclusion, the Trust for Public Land purchased the land in 1990 and, after developing the park, sold it the next year to the Washington State Parks and Recreation Commission. ■

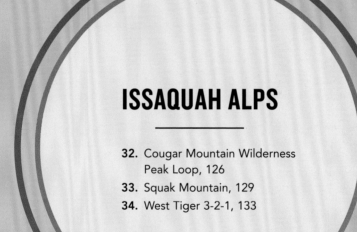

ISSAQUAH ALPS

32. Cougar Mountain Wilderness Peak Loop

RATING	DISTANCE	HIKING TIME
★★★☆☆	4-mile lollipop loop	2 hours

ELEVATION GAIN	HIGH POINT	DIFFICULTY
1,200 feet	1,595 feet	♦♦◇◇◇

BEST SEASON
~~Jan~~ Feb Mar Apr May Jun Jul Aug Sep Oct Nov ~~Dec~~

The Hike

Located mere miles from Seattle, one of the country's major metropolitan areas, this forested walk through deep, dark forest is often deserted. When most folks do the Issaquah Alps, they head to Tiger Mountain or enter Cougar Mountain via the Red Town trailhead. This one starts at Wilderness Creek, on the far east side. And now this excellent hike, formerly known as the Wilderness Peak Trail, has a new name honoring Seattle climbing legend Jim Whittaker, the first American to summit Mount Everest.

Getting There

Head east on Interstate 90 to Exit 15 near Issaquah. Go right (south) on Highway 900 and follow it for 3.2 miles to the signed Cougar

---

PERMITS/CONTACT
None required/Cougar Mountain Regional Wildland Park, (206) 296-4145

MAPS
USGS Bellevue South; Green Trails Cougar Mountain/Squak Mountain 203S;
Cougar Mountain Map (available at the trailhead and at the
King County Parks website)

TRAIL NOTES
Leashed dogs okay; kid-friendly; relative solitude

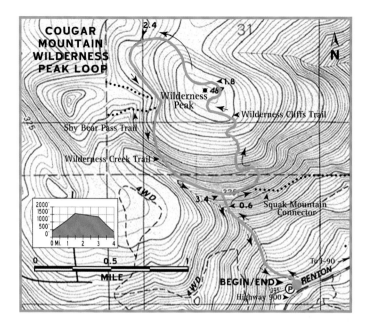

Mountain Regional Wildland Park parking lot on the right. Elevation: 395 feet.

The Trail

Check out the parking lot map kiosk—there are lots of trails; this is just one to whet your appetite—and head up the Whittaker Wilderness Peak Trail. You'll cross Wilderness Creek about 100 yards ahead, just past a box offering free maps. (Thank you.) Climb steadily on a winding single track, gaining a sense of why this is considered the wilderness side of Cougar Mountain. Much of this area has never been logged, and the forest has that primeval feel to it.

At about **0.6** mile, recross Wilderness Creek (*a-gurgle, a-gurgle*) via a couple of wood bridges. At a signed T just beyond, take a right, following a sign for the Gombu Wilderness Cliffs Trail. (Nawang Gombu summited Mount Everest with Jim Whittaker in 1963.)

Wood bridge on Cougar Mountain

The Gombu Wilderness Cliffs Trail also reaches the Wilderness Peak summit, allowing you to make this hike a loop. When the trail forks a few hundred yards ahead, take a left. (To go straight is to access the Squak Mountain Connector Trail, which, as its name suggests, makes it possible to hike from Cougar Mountain right to next-door neighbor Squak Mountain.)

Continue climbing for almost a mile, with rocks and roots offering to trip you up. At **1.8** miles arrive at a T and a sign facing away from you. Take a right, stealing a glance at the sign as you pass, and in about 150 yards, reach Wilderness Peak's summit (1,595 feet). You'll know it's the top not by the grand views (it's completely forested, so there are none), but by the summit register, which invites your comments: "I came. I saw. I conquered," is a good one.

Continue the loop by returning to the sign you just passed and follow its arrow for Shy Bear Pass. From here on, it's downhill. At **2.4** miles arrive at a busy intersection, where it appears that four trails meet within about 20 yards of each other. If you have one of the maps from the trailhead and a taste for more, head off on Shy Bear or Long View or any number of named trails. If continuing on, ignore the first right and go straight ahead to the signed Whittaker Wilderness Peak Trail. Take a left. The trail climbs momentarily, then descends in earnest. About a third of a mile ahead, cross a fun boardwalk through a marshy (and in spring, skunk cabbage–stinky) section of trail. Pass one of several huge boulders in the area that appear to be wearing ill-fitting toupees of sword ferns and moss.

You've licked the lollipop when at **3.4** miles you reach the Wilderness Peak intersection where you took a right before. From here it's a little more than a half-mile back to the parking lot.

Going Farther

A number of trails and trail loops start from Cougar Mountain's Red Town trailhead. To get there, go east on Interstate 90 to Exit 13. Head south on Lakemont Boulevard SE for 3.2 miles to the Red Town trailhead parking lot on the left. ■

33. Squak Mountain

RATING	DISTANCE	HIKING TIME
★★★☆☆	Varies; minimum 7 miles	4 hours
ELEVATION GAIN	**HIGH POINT**	**DIFFICULTY**
1,900 feet	2,000 feet	♦♦♦◇◇
BEST SEASON		
Jan Feb Mar Apr May Jun Jul Aug Sep Oct Nov Dec		

The Hike

Like Jan Brady, Squak Mountain is the one in the middle. Cougar Mountain sits to the west, Tiger Mountain to the east. And just like Jan, Squak Mountain is somewhat underappreciated. The cool cats (Cougar and Tiger) may get bigger crowds, but Squak Mountain has its own charms: a high summit, some legit views, and oodles of trails crisscrossing its 2,500 acres.

Getting There

Head east on Interstate 90 to Exit 15 near Issaquah. Go right (south) on Highway 900 and follow it for 3.4 miles to the Cougar-Mount Squak Corridor parking lot on the left. Elevation: 400 feet.

The Trail

From the parking lot managed by King County Parks, stop and check out the detailed map for Squak Mountain. You'll see a number of trails in the Cougar-Squak Corridor and many more in neighboring Squak Mountain State Park. In all, 2,500 acres are spread out over the mountainside.

Grab a free map (thanks, King County Parks) and follow Margaret's Way, a 2.7-mile trail that climbs 1,300 vertical feet to the Chybinski Loop Trail. From there the mountaintop ridge sprawls over 1.5 miles, culminating with a tower-topped summit at 2,000 feet.

Margaret's Way is a relatively new trail named for Margaret MacLeod, a park planner who was instrumental in securing land for hiking use in the Issaquah Alps. Thanks to thousands of volunteer hours donated by Washington Trails Association, the route was completed in 2015 and is a delightful romp through mixed forest, ravines, and streams, with an eventual steep climb to the ridgeline.

Margaret's Way starts on a gravel roadway that switchbacks up the western flank of Squak Mountain. About 100 yards up the road, watch for the first of what feels like hundreds of "Margaret's Way" signs that take you off the road and onto the trail. You'll continue this road-trail dance for a while, with "Margaret's Way" signs directing your moves.

At **0.7** mile, you'll reach a viewpoint. From here the trail turns sharply, leaving the road for good, utilizing old, decaying logging roads and hand-built trails to continue its pathway ever upward. It's an interesting journey, one that leaves the traffic noise of busy Highway 900

PERMITS/CONTACT
None required/King County Parks, (206) 477-4527

MAPS
USGS Bellevue South; Green Trails Cougar Mountain/Squak Mountain 203S; Cougar-Squak-Tiger Mountain Corridor map (available at the trailhead and at King County Parks' website)

TRAIL NOTES
Leashed dogs okay; kid-friendly; nice views

Hikers climb along the Squak Mountain trail

quickly behind. Even though the bustling, booming metropolis is mere miles away, you'll quickly feel like you're away from it all amid the moss-covered forest.

At **1.0** mile, you'll reach a lovely maple-tree-topped ridge with partial views of Cougar Mountain to the west. From here, the route rolls briefly downhill into a sometimes-wet ravine before resuming a steep but manageable climb on switchbacks through deepening forest. The higher you climb, the cooler it gets—funny how that works. The ridge top breezes increase and at **2.7** miles, you reach the Chybinski Loop Trail. Now it's decision time. Your choices: go for a quick view, go another 1.5 miles to the summit, or do both.

If you choose the view, take a right and walk about 30 yards to a well-signed trail junction. Follow signs to the right for Debbie's View and in about a mile, you'll find a delightful vantage point south, with Mount Rainier staring you in the face. Hang out on the comfy bench, have a bite, and return the same way, completing your round trip at 7 miles.

But some of us must get to the top, even though in this case the top is crowned with communication towers. To continue your climb, return to the trail junction where you left the Chybinski Loop Trail and take the West Peak Trail east. You'll climb about 200 feet of elevation over a

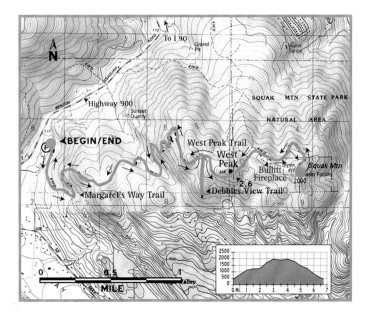

quarter-mile to the summit of West Peak, a thickly forested high point. It's fairly uninspiring and easy to miss in the deep, dark forest. You'll know you're there when you see the remains of an old building, now completely collapsed and slowly returning to Mother Earth.

Onward to the top: Follow the West Peak trail down 0.3 mile to another well-signed trail junction, and go right on the Bullit Fireplace Trail. Climb steeply for about 50 yards and you'll find said fireplace, along with a picnic table, sitting in a clearing. It's what remains of the former summer home of the Bullit family, who donated the original 600 acres of land on Squak Mountain to Washington State Parks.

Just past the fireplace, bear left at another trail junction and drop a couple hundred feet over a third of a mile to the Central Peak Trail. Go right up another third of a mile to tower-topped Squak Mountain's Central Peak. And by all means, let out "Squak!" for good measure. Congratulations—you've hit the turnaround point. Your car is 4.2 miles back the way you came.

Going Farther

There are many ways to extend your hike in the maze of trails on the north and east sides of Squak Mountain, including several loop options. One possibility is to head back down the Central Peak Trail on the mountain's north flank, following signs for the West Access Trail. Once on the West Access Trail, you'll descend to Highway 900; from there, carefully walk the busy road back to your car 0.7 mile up the hill to the southwest. ∎

34. West Tiger 3-2-1

RATING	DISTANCE	HIKING TIME
★★★☆☆	7.0 miles round-trip	4 hours
ELEVATION GAIN	HIGH POINT	DIFFICULTY
2,600 feet	2,948 feet	◆◆◆◇
BEST SEASON		
Jan Feb Mar Apr May Jun Jul Aug Sep Oct Nov Dec		

The Hike

Like a Whitman Sampler, this route gives you a sample of Tiger Mountain's many flavors. You've got your people-pleasin' West Tiger No. 3 with its popular, easily approachable mountaintop, and your obscure other summits (West Tigers No. 2 and No. 1) mere yards away and likely deserted. And for laughs, we throw in the Section Line Trail, which gains more than 1,300 feet in less than a mile.

Getting There

Head east on Interstate 90 to Exit 20, about 2.0 miles east of Issaquah. Take a right on 270th Avenue SE and then a quick right on SE 79th St. (Follow the sign for Lake Tradition through a gate and onto a gravel roadway.) Continue 0.8 mile to the West Tiger Mountain and Tradition Plateau trailhead, also known as the High Point parking lot. Elevation: 520 feet.

The Trail

Tiger is the largest of the three Issaquah Alps—Tiger, Cougar, and Squak Mountains—with more than 70 miles of trails crisscrossing it. (Although if you include Rattlesnake Mountain as one of the Alps, as some people do, I suppose Tiger Mountain would have a fight on its hands.) It ain't exactly virgin forest—much of it was clear-cut in the 1930s and 1970s—and it's still a working forest managed by the Department of Natural Resources. Still, Tiger Mountain's mixed leafy-evergreen forest, carpeted with ferns and wildflowers, offers terrific hiking, wilderness opportunities, and some pretty decent views. It's all the more amazing given its proximity to the Seattle metropolitan area. When the higher trails are covered in snow, head here.

From the kiosk at the southwest end of the parking lot, follow the sign for trails and enter the forest. The pathway is a gravel path built to handle the masses. You're looking for the Bus Trail—follow the main pathway for a couple hundred yards until you come to an intersection for the "Around the Lake Trail, Bus Trail Link." The Tiger Mountain and West Tiger Mountain Trails go straight. You'll take a right and walk for about 150 yards, crossing a creek on a spiffy bridge until you hit the intersection for the Nook Trail. Go left here—this is the last of your early turns. You'll climb steadily through thick forest on the Nook Trail, a pleasant walk in the woods that has far fewer hikers than the West Tiger Mountain trail.

PERMITS/CONTACT
Discover Pass required/Department of Natural Resources, South Puget Sound Region Natural Areas Manager, (360) 825-1631

MAPS
USGS Fall City; Green Trails Tiger Mountain 204S

TRAIL NOTES
Leashed dogs okay; nice views

with decent views through the growing mountaintop forest of Lake Washington, Seattle, Puget Sound, and the Olympic Range beyond, it's not surprising. A small clearing with a couple of large sitting rocks makes for a nice place to picnic. Turn around and return via the slightly more tame West Tiger No. 3 Trail, or continue on to the next two summits on your agenda and save your picnic for the way back. Just so you know, West Tiger No. 3 is the only summit with a view.

Head straight across the bare summit area in the direction of West Tiger No. 2 (the close hill to the southeast wearing the cell tower tiara) and find a trail switchbacking downhill into the trees. After about a quarter-mile, begin the short ascent to your second summit, passing through another Tiger Mountain Trail intersection on the way. At **2.9** miles emerge from the forest at the forested summit at the foot of the cell tower tiara. Elevation: 2,757 feet.

Two summits down, one to go. Find the dirt road to the right and drop about 200 feet over the next quarter-mile until you reach a gate. Just beyond the gate, take the left fork, a dirt road that climbs steeply to the summit of West Tiger No. 1. At **3.5** miles reach The Hiker's Hut. Because of the communication towers here, signs warn you to stay away, so you're not allowed near the actual top. You're close enough, however, to give yourself credit for your third summit of the day—West Tiger No. 1. Elevation: 2,948 feet.

Return the same way you came.

Going Farther

On your way back, you might want to consider going down the West Tiger Trail. The trail is busier, but the descent is easier on the knees than the steep fall-line drop of the Section Line Trail, making your return trip 3.1 miles from West Tiger No. 3. ■

NORTH BEND

35. Rattlesnake Mountain (Snoqualmie Point to Grand Prospect)

RATING	DISTANCE	HIKING TIME
★★★☆☆	**9.8 miles round-trip**	**6 hours**

ELEVATION GAIN	HIGH POINT	DIFFICULTY
2,300 feet	**3,100 feet**	◆◆◆◇◇

BEST SEASON
Jan Feb **Mar Apr May Jun Jul Aug Sep Oct Nov** Dec

The Hike

Next time you're in North Bend, take your eyes off Mount Si for a sec and look south and practically straight up. That massive forested ridge wearing the cell tower tiara is Rattlesnake Mountain, and here's the trail that takes you to the top. Views are huge—to as far away as Mount Baker and along Bandera Ridge into the Alpine Lakes Wilderness.

Getting There

Go east on Interstate 90 to Exit 27 near North Bend. Turn right (south) off the exit. Go 0.3 mile and turn right into the trailhead parking lot at Snoqualmie Point. Elevation: 980 feet.

PERMITS/CONTACT
Department of Natural Resources, South Puget Sound Region

MAPS
USGS North Bend; Green Trails Rattlesnake Mountain 205S

TRAIL NOTES
Leashed dogs okay; kid-friendly—at lower reaches of trail; great Snoqualmie Valley views

Mount Si and North Bend from Rattlesnake Mountain

The Trail

Admittedly, this is not a trail where you put your mind on autopilot and just go. It's a connection of trails and former logging roads that traverse the mountain's spine and, therefore, requires you to stay alert to ensure that you don't stray down a road or trail to nowhere. That said, however, it's darn easy to follow. All connections are well signed—really well signed—and as time goes on, the 11-mile Rattlesnake Mountain Trail from Snoqualmie Point to Rattlesnake Lake will follow much less road and be nearly all trail. Thanks to several organizations, this wooded route continues to mature as Mother Nature returns some clear-cuts to forests and roads give way to trails. Kudos to the Mountains to Sound Greenway, Issaquah Alps, and Washington Trails Association for all their hard work.

Find the trailhead sign on the right and begin climbing up an old logging road for about a quarter-mile to the Rattlesnake Mountain sign and one of those hiker-only gates that encourage bicyclists and equestrians to find somewhere else to play. (You'll come to these gates throughout the route and some of them are so narrow, even

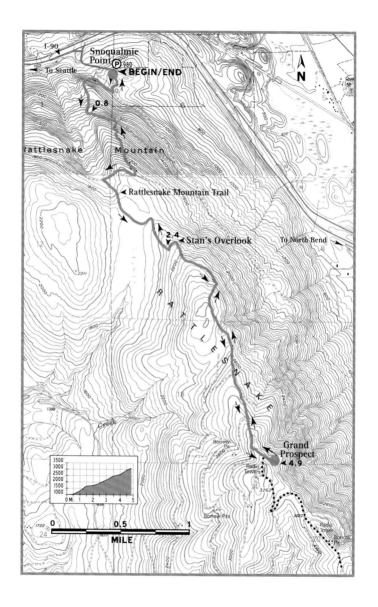

Snoqualmie
Point

I-90

To Seattle

P 980

BEGIN/END

0.8

Rattlesnake   Mountain

Rattlesnake Mountain Trail

2.4   Stan's Overlook

To North Bend

R
A
T
T
L
E
S
N
A
K
E

Creek

Borrow
Pit

Grand
Prospect

4.9

Radio
Towers

Borrow Pits

Radio
Tower

Borrow
Pit

3500
3000
2500
2000
1500
1000

0 Mi.   1   2   3   4   5

0   0.5   1
MILE

N

the skinniest hiker would have trouble squeezing through.) Now on the trail, climb steadily through deciduous forest populated with the occasional massive cedar stump that belies the forest's past. Yes, you can hear the freeway, but just ahead, through openings in the trees, you have the first views down to the Snoqualmie Valley, across to Mount Si, and even north to Mount Baker on clear days.

You'll pass a creek on your right and come to an unsigned intersection at **0.8** mile. Go straight on an old roadbed for about 300 yards. Turn right as the trail climbs into a recovering clear-cut slope that is returning to forest, with some semi-open views. And while you're at it, you'll spy pileated woodpeckers, of which I saw two in a single morning once on this trail. The trail crosses a number of logging roads, and a huge Rattlesnake Mountain Trail sign and hiker-only gate directs you back to the trail on the other side.

Continue in this fashion in and out of forest, some older than others, for several miles. At about **2.4** miles reach a logging road (the trail continues on the other side), but before continuing on the trail, follow the road to the left for about 100 yards to Stan's Overlook (elevation: 2,100 feet). There's a picnic table and a couple of benches at an open vista point that offers terrific views of the whole valley. Mount Si appears gi-normous! Note how the smaller forested hills to the west of Si resemble rolled-up sock balls left under the blankets on a bed. This is a good turnaround point for those with less time or inclination for the top.

Back on the tread, the trail swings around to the back (southwest) side of the mountain and for the first time the freeway sounds disappear. Just ahead the trail enters dense, dark DNR forest and couldn't be any more different than the trail's earlier parts. Go slowly because although the trail is mostly easy to follow, there are points where you could very easily lose it. Keep your eyes open for red flagging on the trees.

The trail roller-coasters up and down for a bit, crosses a damp creek area, and resumes climbing. Soon enough, the Rattlesnake Trail signs return as you once again pop in and out of forest. At **4.9** miles reach the Grand Prospect. Benches and an interpretive sign welcome you, as do splendiferous Snoqualmie Valley, North Cascade, Mount Si,

Defiance Ridge, and Central Cascade views. You'll note that Si is not so big from this angle; it's more the frontispiece for a massif that includes Mount Teneriffe and Green Mountain, both of which tower over Si.

Return the same way, but on the way down, follow signs for Snoqualmie Point.

Going Farther

Snoqualmie Point Park near the trailhead is an excellent place to rest and have a picnic after your hike, with great views of Mount Si and North Bend. If you want to hike the entire 10.2-mile Rattlesnake Mountain Trail end to end from Snoqualmie Point to Rattlesnake Lake, park one car at the Rattlesnake Ledge (Hike 40) trailhead and the other at the Snoqualmie Point trailhead. Either way gains about the same amount of elevation. ■

36. Snoqualmie Falls

RATING ★★ ☆☆☆	DISTANCE **1 mile round-trip**	HIKING TIME **1 hour**
ELEVATION GAIN **370 feet**	HIGH POINT **440 feet**	DIFFICULTY ◆ ◇◇◇◇
BEST SEASON		
Jan **Feb Mar Apr May Jun Jul Aug Sep Oct Nov** Dec		

The Hike

Yes, it's touristy, but seeing a 270-foot horsetail of water plunging into the Snoqualmie River below is still impressive as heck. Although not nearly as wide, Snoqualmie's falls are 100 feet higher than Niagara's. And those falls were never featured in the TV show *Twin Peaks*, as these were. Follow this trail and be amazed by the power of water plus gravity.

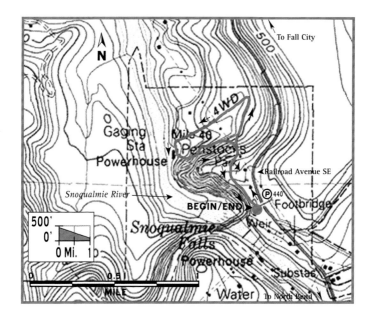

Getting There

Head east on Interstate 90 to Exit 25 near Snoqualmie. Go north on the Snoqualmie Parkway (Highway 18) for about 3.6 miles to a T intersection with Railroad Avenue (Highway 202). Turn left and continue for about 0.6 mile to a roundabout, and follow signs for Highway 202. The falls are on the left side of the road, but park in the signed lot on

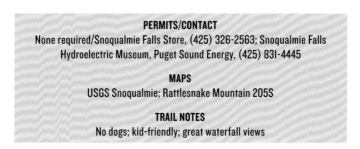

PERMITS/CONTACT
None required/Snoqualmie Falls Store, (425) 326-2563; Snoqualmie Falls Hydroelectric Museum, Puget Sound Energy, (425) 831-4445

MAPS
USGS Snoqualmie; Rattlesnake Mountain 205S

TRAIL NOTES
No dogs; kid-friendly; great waterfall views

River meets gravity at Snoqualmie Falls

the right (it's free) and use the walkway over Railroad Avenue to get to the falls. Elevation: 440 feet.

The Trail

From the parking lot cross over always busy Highway 202 using a covered pedestrian walkway, and check out the views of the falls from the walkway overlook. If it's raining, continue a few yards to a covered observation platform, where when the wind is right, the spray hits you smack in the face, adding a tactile aspect to the experience. That's the Salish Lodge, a posh resort, perched there at the edge and looking like it's about to tumble over. (The rest of the man-made stuff there is part of the two on-site Puget Power plants that convert some of the falls' mega-flow into enough electricity to serve sixteen thousand homes.)

For the riverside views and experience, continue along the walkway past the gift shop, espresso stand, and restrooms (this is the only trail in this guide with a gift shop and espresso stand at the trailhead) to the sign for River Trail. Truthfully, the trail itself ain't much—just a wide, gravel road through second-growth forest that drops more than 300 feet in about a half-mile—but you're probably here for the falls anyway.

Once near the bottom, go left and follow signs for the boardwalk. (If you want to reach the river, go right and follow signs that say "river access," but you won't be able to see the falls from that area.) The trail to the falls reaches a fenced boardwalk (it feels like you're in a cage) along Power Plant 2. You saw Power Plant 1 higher up near the top of the falls. Follow the boardwalk for about 100 yards, sensing as you walk the theme that the many signs warning you to stay on the boardwalk and away from the base of the falls reflect, until at about **0.5** mile when you reach the end of the boardwalk. The straight-on falls view is truly stunning and it's understandable why 1.5 million people flock here each year.

At one time, it was possible to skirt the barricades and reach the shoreline near the falls, but Puget Sound Energy has improved its safety fencing, making it nearly impossible to get closer. Drone aircraft, once allowed at the falls, are now prohibited (if you were hoping to get that magical photo or video).

Return the same way. ■

37. Little Si

RATING	DISTANCE	HIKING TIME
★★★☆☆	3.8 miles round-trip	2.5 hours
ELEVATION GAIN	HIGH POINT	DIFFICULTY
1,200 feet	1,576 feet	♦♦◊◊◊

BEST SEASON
Jan Feb Mar Apr May Jun Jul Aug Sep Oct Nov Dec

The Hike

It must be tough being Little Si, always literally in Mount Si's shadow. But this is a great trail in its own right and one lusted after by those of the rock-climbing persuasion. At 1,576 feet, Little Si's summit is reachable pretty much year-round and offers great views toward the Snoqualmie Valley, Rattlesnake Mountain, and (oh yeah) Mount Si. On weekends expect crowds.

Getting There

From Interstate 90, take Exit 32 in North Bend. Head north on 436th Avenue SE for 0.6 mile to North Bend Way. Turn left and follow it for 0.2 mile to Mount Si Road. The well-marked trailhead is 0.6 mile ahead on the left. Elevation: 490 feet.

PERMITS/CONTACT
Discover Pass required/Department of Natural Resources South Puget Sound
Region, (360) 825-1631

MAPS
USGS North Bend; Green Trails Mount Si NRCA 206S

TRAIL NOTES
Leashed dogs okay; kid-friendly; great valley views

The Trail

The trail climbs steeply—and a bit rockily—at first but soon enters the forest, where it seems to meander for a bit, not really in a rush to do the climbing thing or, it seems, to even get you to where you want to go. You'll come to several intersections, all of which thankfully are marked with signs pointing the way to Little Si. At about **1.0** mile, the trail moves deeper into the ravine between Little Si and its big brother to the east. The forest deepens, road noises from North Bend quiet, and the hike grows more pleasant with every step.

The trail resumes climbing through cool, dark, second-growth forest populated by mossy boulders the size of tool sheds and voices that seem to be coming out of thin air. Actually, they're from rock climbers high on the wall to your left. Little Si is popular with rock jocks, and although the trees and terrain prevent you from seeing most of them, their voices carry. Right in here you'll pass a bench dedicated to the memory of Doug Hansen, who died in

Cool, dark forest on the way to Little Si

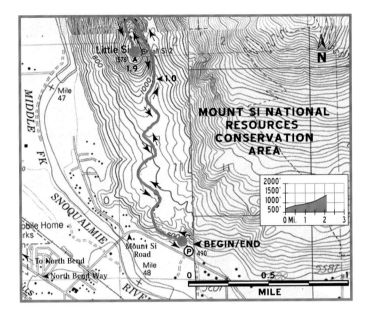

1996 on Mount Everest during the tragic expedition made famous by Jon Krakauer's book *Into Thin Air*.

The trail climbs steeply over the next mile or so as it travels along the glacier-carved valley between the Si's. (Yes, it's occurred to me, too, that if there were a bridge between the two it'd be called the Bridge of Si's.) From time to time, views through the trees open up revealing Mount Si. The last half-mile climbs steeply and can be a bit rough, with plenty of rocks and exposed roots. Be careful, as it can be extremely slippery when wet. At **1.9** miles, reach the craggy top and revel in 360-degree views of the Snoqualmie Valley, Rattlesnake Mountain and Ledge, Mount Washington and the start of the Central Cascades, and, of course, Mount Si dominating all to the northeast.

Return the same way. ∎

38. Mount Si

RATING	DISTANCE	HIKING TIME
★★★★	8.0 miles round-trip	5 hours

ELEVATION GAIN	HIGH POINT	DIFFICULTY
3,400 feet	3,980 feet	◆◆◆◆

BEST SEASON
Jan Feb **Mar Apr May Jun Jul Aug Sep Oct Nov** Dec

The Hike

It's the most popular trail in the state. It's steep as all heck. It was featured in the 1990s TV show *Twin Peaks*. Each year, more than eighty thousand hikers, trail runners, and climbers form a conga line to the summit. So why should you hike Si? Because the views from the top are out of this world—Mount Rainier and all of Western Washington appear as if on a buffet table spread out especially for you. And just because it's popular doesn't necessarily mean it's lame; after all, the Beatles proved to be pretty good, and who was more popular than they?

Getting There

Head east on Interstate 90 to Exit 32 in North Bend. Go north on 436th Avenue for about 0.5 mile to North Bend Way. Turn left and in about 0.3 mile, turn right on Mount Si Road. Follow it for 2.4 miles to the well-signed trailhead parking lot on the left. Elevation: 660 feet.

The Trail

After browsing the found items on display near the trailhead kiosk—how *does* one lose a pair of shorts?—find the obvious trail, seemingly mocking you with its flatness for the first 50 yards. Ah, but such frivolous flatness ends in a moment when the real climbing—and the real Mount Si—begins. At one time, this trail was a rocky, root-riddled mess, but some exceptional trail work in recent years has smoothed out the path. The trail is still just as steep, but strategically placed rocks and logs make the climbing much more efficient. By the

The view clearly displays why this hike is so popular

PERMITS/CONTACT
Discover Pass required/Washington State Department of Natural Resources
South Puget Sound Region, (360) 825-1631

MAPS
USGS Chester Morse Lake, Mount Si; Green Trails Mount Si NRCA 206S

TRAIL NOTES
Leashed dogs okay; spectacular views; big crowds; steep

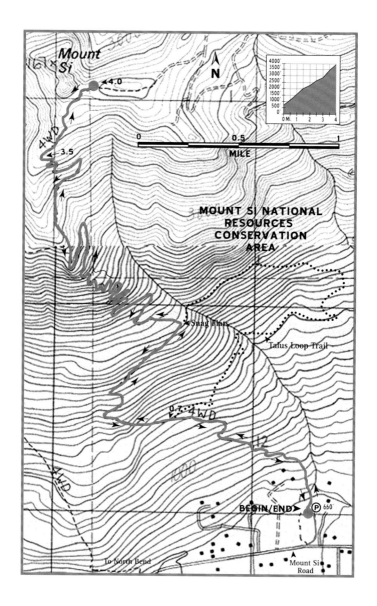

Mount Si

N

MOUNT SI NATIONAL
RESOURCES
CONSERVATION
AREA

Snag Flats

Talus Loop Trail

0   0.5   1

MILE

4.0

3.5

0.7

4WD

4WD

BEGIN/END ⓅP 660'

To North Bend

Mount Si
Road

way, the mountain is named for Josiah Merritt, an old Snoqualmie Valley homesteader, and not for the sounds of weariness you may find yourself emitting from time to time on this trail.

At **0.7** mile continue straight where the signed Talus Loop Trail heads off to the right. Just past **1.0** mile, views open up to the south and, if it's clear, include a nice picture-window view of Mount Rainier. Just before **2.0** miles, reach Snag Flats, a 100-yard stretch that, given all the uphill hiking you've done to this point, will feel like you're running downhill at free-fall speed. Take a few moments to marvel at some massive fire-scorched firs that over the centuries have survived multiple conflagrations. Families with small kids might want to make this a picnic or turnaround point.

If you're continuing on, climb some more. And more. And more. And even more. Count the number of individuals you come across training for Rainier ascents, obvious by their huge packs, ice axes, and plastic boots. At **3.5** miles the forest opens up once again to the south, revealing even more impressive mountain views. Stop and gawk or, if you can, wait a half-mile for the top. At **4.0** miles reach Haystack Basin, a talus-strewn shoulder that amazes with 180-degree views guaranteed to knock your Smartwool socks off. You've done it! You've made it to the top of Mount Si! (You and 99,000 others—the estimated number of people who make it to the top annually.)

Eat and drink while you enjoy the spectacular Snoqualmie Valley–Mount Rainier–Puget Sound–Seattle skyline–Olympic Mountain panorama. When you've had enough, return the same way, no doubt wondering if there's enough ice in your freezer for all that your knees are going to need tonight. ■

39. Talus Loop Trail

RATING	DISTANCE	HIKING TIME
★★★☆☆	3.7-mile lollipop loop	2 hours

ELEVATION GAIN	HIGH POINT	DIFFICULTY
1,420 feet	2,120 feet	◆◆◆◇◇

BEST SEASON
Jan Feb **Mar Apr May Jun Jul Aug Sep Oct Nov** Dec

The Hike

Although this loop on Mount Si's southeast flank takes you only about halfway up the mountain, it offers some grand Snoqualmie Valley–Central Cascade views. Compared with the Mount Si trail's waste-no-time march to the summit, this is a kinder, gentler foray into the forest.

Getting There

Head east on Interstate 90 to Exit 32 in North Bend. Drive north on 436th Avenue SE for about 0.5 mile to North Bend Way. Turn left and in about 0.3 mile turn right onto Mount Si Road. The trailhead parking lot is 2.4 miles ahead on the left. Elevation: 660 feet.

The Trail

Sure, Mount Si is crowded, but on weekdays . . . it's still crowded. That's why this Talus Loop is a nice variation. Get in line and start by

PERMITS/CONTACT
Discover Pass required/Department of Natural Resources South Puget Sound Region, (360) 825-1631

MAPS
USGS North Bend; Green Trails Mount Si NRCA 206S

TRAIL NOTES
Leashed dogs okay; kid-friendly; great views

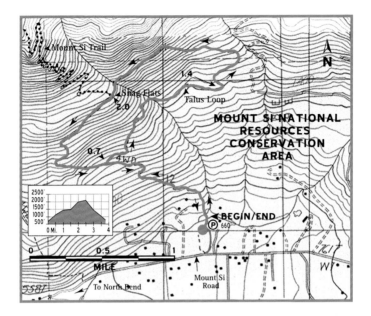

hiking the rocky, root-riddled, densely wooded, elevation-gobbling Mount Si Trail for about 0.7 mile to the signed intersection with the Talus Loop Trail. Go right.

Immediately, the trail quits its hard-core climbing behavior and the forest opens out a bit. The trail meanders along the mountainside, climbing gradually with a few ups and downs for good measure as it wanders east. At about **1.4** miles the trail regains some of it Si-esque prowess and resumes climbing steeply up the first of several rocky, bouldery stretches. A couple narrow ledges offer semi-obstructed views through the trees to Mount Washington and the valley below. Better views are just ahead

In about one-third of a mile reach the reason the trail earns its name—a broad talus slope with terrific views of the Snoqualmie River valley and the line of peaks on either side. You'll see Mailbox Peak and Defiance Ridge on the north side, and Mount Washington, McClellan Butte, and on down the line on the south side. Find a rock (there are

Talus Loop offers a gentler take on Mount Si

plenty around), take a load off, and admire the views. Sure, maybe you didn't climb to the top like the Mount Si summit-or-busters, but hey, you had a bit more serenity, you're enjoying views that are almost as good, and tonight your knees will thank you for not putting them through the 3,200 feet of downhill pounding those summiteers will experience.

Once across the talus the trail ducks back into the woods and climbs steeply for a few hundred yards. Just after a sharp bend by a creek, at **2.0** miles, the trail intersects once again with the Mount Si Trail about a mile farther along and 800 feet higher than where you left it. Go left on the Mount Si Trail and head back to the parking lot at what feels like free-fall speed. Along the way, stop and take a gander at the Snag Flats Interpretive Area, a short stretch so named because of the ginormous snags, remnants of the mountain's last old-growth trees that were killed in the 1920s in a forest fire.

Going Farther
The Talus Loop Trail is also the trailhead for Mount Si (Hike 38). ■

40. Rattlesnake Ledge

RATING	DISTANCE	HIKING TIME
★★★★☆	4.0 miles round-trip	2 hours

ELEVATION GAIN	HIGH POINT	DIFFICULTY
1,100 feet	2,079 feet	◆◆◇◇◇

BEST SEASON
Jan Feb Mar Apr May Jun Jul Aug Sep Oct Nov Dec

The Hike

This trail to a dramatic viewpoint looking down on Rattlesnake Lake is popular—as in way crowded on spring, summer, and fall weekends. Only the Mount Si Trail, across the Snoqualmie Valley, is more accommodating. Once up top, stay back from the ledge unless you can fly. It's 1,100 feet straight down.

Getting There

From Interstate 90 take Exit 32 in North Bend. Head south on 436th Avenue SE (which turns into Cedar Falls Road SE) for 2.7 miles and park at the signed parking lot to the right. Elevation: 920 feet.

The Trail

The old Rattlesnake Ledge Trail climbed 1,100 feet in 1.3 miles. That's steep stuff. It was a series of seemingly endless switchbacks

PERMITS/CONTACT
None required/Department of Natural Resources, South Puget Sound Region, (360) 825-1631; Cedar River Watershed Education Center, (206) 733-9421 or (425) 831-6780

MAPS
USGS North Bend; Green Trails Rattlesnake Mountain 205S

TRAIL NOTES
Leashed dogs okay—but with deadly drop-offs at the ledge, it might not be a good idea; kid-friendly—but again, hold onto them at the top

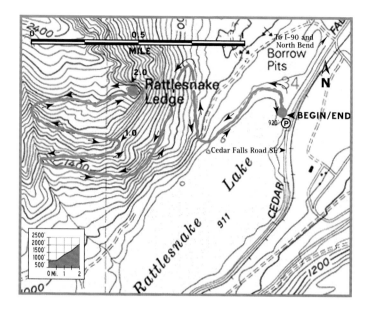

that, judging from the condition of the trail, many hikers couldn't resist the temptation to cut in order to head straight up the mountain, thus eroding the hillside in the process.

No more. The wide, reworked trail (circa 2003) is 0.75 mile longer to the top, but it's smoother and much more accommodating, ultimately making this hike easier. A variety of volunteer groups and agencies helped rebuild the trail and it has paid off nicely as the years of boot prints continue to add up.

From the parking lot follow signs around the lake for the trailhead, which is just up from the lake's west shore. Follow a service road briefly to the trailhead with a map showing the route. The trail begins climbing (gently) through a forest of alder, fir, and hemlock, with your shins and ankles tickled by sword ferns, salal, and Oregon grape. At about **1.0** mile an opening in the trees provides the first views south toward the Cedar River Education Center and, when the clouds allow, Mount Rainier. But don't get too excited; the super views are

Eyeing the I-90 peaks from Rattlesnake Ledge

from the top and that's only a mile away. Back on the trail and back in the woods you go.

A little less than a mile later, reach the top of the ridge at **2.0** miles with open north-facing views and a signed intersection. To go left is to continue on the Rattlesnake Mountain (Snoqualmie Point to Grand Prospect) Trail (Hike 35); go right for about 100 yards along the open rocky ridge for the ledge. The spectacular 270-degree vista includes more forested folds and ridges and rocky peaks and canyons than you could ever count. Mount Washington, gateway to the Central Cascades, rises skyward to the east, like a sentry keeping watch over Chester Morse Lake and Seattle's water supply. To the north Mount Si keeps its eye on the entire Snoqualmie Valley. And directly below, just 1,100 feet of air away, is Rattlesnake Lake, its paddlers and splashers looking more like twigs and bugs in a puddle. Sit back, relax, and take in the views.

Return the same way.

Going Farther

The Rattlesnake Mountain Trail that traverses the Rattlesnake Mountain Ridge can be accessed via the same trailhead as the Rattlesnake Ledge Trail or at Snoqualmie Point. ■

41. John Wayne Pioneer Trail– Iron Horse State Park

RATING	DISTANCE	HIKING TIME
★★★★☆	**Varies, many options**	**Varies**

ELEVATION GAIN	HIGH POINT	DIFFICULTY
Minimal	**2,600 feet**	◆◇◇◇◇

BEST SEASON
Jan Feb **Mar Apr May Jun Jul Aug Sep Oct Nov** Dec

The Hike

Reaching from Rattlesnake Lake near North Bend to Vantage on the Columbia River, this old Chicago–Milwaukee–St. Paul Pacific Railroad rail trail makes for great day hiking. (Not the whole thing, of course.) Numerous trailheads along the trail's 100-mile length offer variety in a big way—past waterfalls, below cliffs peopled with rock climbers, over high trestles with spectacular mountain views, not to mention *through* the Cascades; see the Snoqualmie Tunnel (Hike 61). Best yet, as an old rail line, the hills, such as they are, are minimal. (Note: Snoqualmie Tunnel closes in the winter.)

Getting There

Here are five access points to the John Wayne Pioneer Trail from Rattlesnake Lake, the trail's western terminus near North Bend, to the Hyak trailhead, where the trail reaches its highest point near Snoqualmie Pass. Keep in mind that the trail climbs gradually from west to east. Elevation for the Rattlesnake Lake section: 900 feet; elevation for Hyak: 2,600 feet.

Rattlesnake Lake. From Interstate 90 east of North Bend, take Exit 32. Go south on 436th Avenue SE, which becomes Cedar Falls Road SE. The first of several Rattlesnake Lake parking lots is about 2.9 miles from I-90. Note: There is a John Wayne Pioneer Trail–Iron Horse State Park parking lot just up the road from Rattlesnake Lake, but parking there costs $5. Parking at Rattlesnake Lake is free.

Interstate 90, Exit 38. Park at the Twin Falls Natural Area parking lot, just off freeway Exit 38. From the exit go right and park just ahead. Follow a short access trail for about 0.3 mile to an intersection with the John Wayne Trail.

Interstate 90, Exit 42. Park at the McClellan Butte trailhead, about 0.5 mile south of the exit at the end of Forest Road 5500-101. Follow the trail for about 0.5 mile to the John Wayne Trail.

Interstate 90, Exit 47. Park at the Annette Lake trailhead, about 0.3 mile from the freeway exit off FR 55. Follow the Annette Lake Trail (not Asahel Curtis Nature Trail) for about 0.7 mile to the intersection with the John Wayne Trail.

Hyak trailhead. From I-90 just east of Snoqualmie Pass, take Exit 54. At the end of the exit ramp, take a right and then a quick left onto Spur 906. (Follow signs for Snoqualmie Tunnel.) Go right in 0.5 mile; the Hyak trailhead parking lot is just ahead.

The Trail

From the above access points, the trail can be hiked for any distance (just turn around when you've had enough), or use a car shuttle for point-to-point walking. Here's what to expect along the way, going from west to east.

Rattlesnake Lake to Twin Falls. Here, interpretive signs at the trailhead fill you in on a bit of the rail trail's history, such as the fact

PERMITS/CONTACT
Discover Pass required for parking at Twin Falls and Hyak trailheads;
Northwest Forest Pass required for parking at McClellan Butte and
Annette Lake trailheads/Lake Easton State Park
(they take calls for Iron Horse State Park), (509) 656-2230

MAPS
Multiple USGS maps; Green Trails Rattlesnake Mountain 205S, Bandera 206,
Snoqualmie Pass 207, Snoqualmie Pass Gateway 207S

TRAIL NOTES
Leashed dogs okay; kid-friendly; historic; bicycles okay

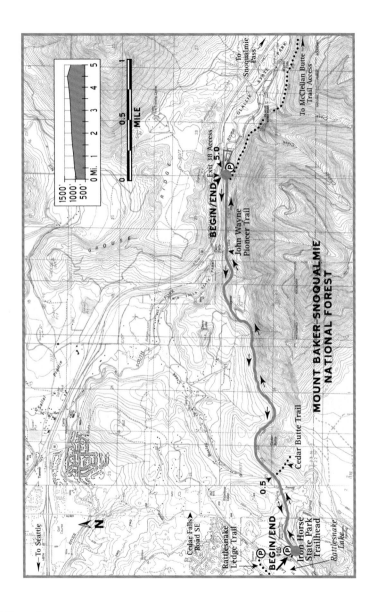

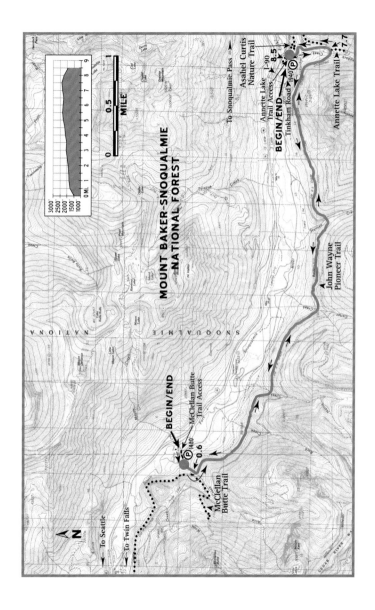

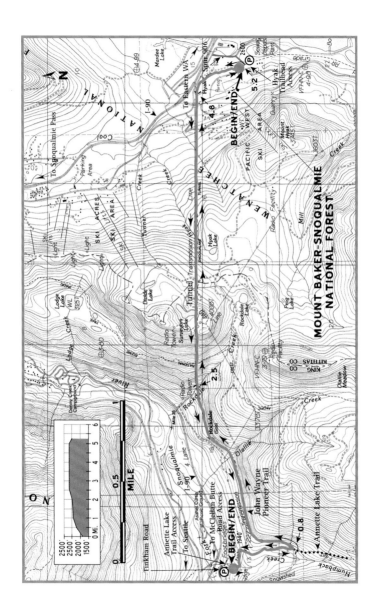

One of the John Wayne Pioneer Trail's new trestles

that trains first started making their way via this line in 1908, and that it was the last of the transcontinental railroads to be built. Nine years later, however, it became the first electrified transcontinental railway in the country. In the 1930s and 1940s the Milwaukee Road Snow Train took passengers from Seattle to the Snoqualmie Ski Bowl, an early ski area. It was a two-hour trip from Seattle, two-and-a-half from Tacoma. Today the trail is named for John Wayne because, according to an interpretive sign that's actually near the Hyak trailhead, for many the Duke symbolizes the "positive spirit of the West." As for the trail itself, much of it along this stretch is peaceful and tree lined. You pass the Cedar Butte trailhead (Hike 42) and when the trees open, views to Mount Si and the whole Mailbox Peak to Bandera Mountain Ridge and beyond are yours.

Exit 38 to Exit 42. Rock climbers and trestles sum up this portion. Here the trail passes below the cliffs of the popular Exit 38 rock-climbing area and across trestles with views far down to various creekbeds. There are open views across to the I-90 corridor and up to Defiance Ridge.

Exit 42 to Exit 47. More trestles, and more mountain views as the rail trail gradually gains elevation on its way to Snoqualmie Pass.

Exit 47 to Hyak. After about 1.5 miles of light and mountains and airy views, there is darkness like you wouldn't believe—the Snoqualmie Tunnel (Hike 61). Bring a jacket and a headlamp with extra batteries; it's cold and pitch dark inside.

Going Farther

Add parts of the Upper Snoqualmie Valley Trail for a John Wayne rail-trail walk that starts in Snoqualmie or North Bend. And, of course, the John Wayne Trail continues east to the Columbia River. ∎

42. Cedar Butte

RATING	DISTANCE	HIKING TIME
★★★☆☆	4.0-mile lollipop loop	2 hours
ELEVATION GAIN	**HIGH POINT**	**DIFFICULTY**
950 feet	1,860 feet	◆◆◇◇◇

BEST SEASON											
Jan	Feb	Mar	Apr	May	Jun	Jul	Aug	Sep	Oct	Nov	Dec

The Hike

This prominent bump, known as one of the North Bend Blobs, rises from the plain between the Issaquah Alps and the Central Cascades. The much-improved trail boasts great views of both the Alps and Cascades, as well as north toward Mount Si, on which you can almost see the mountain sag and sigh under the weight of its eighty thousand annual hikers. Cedar Butte also sports a spur trail that passes the Boxley Blowout, site of the 1918 Cedar River reservoir leak that washed away the tiny town of Edgewick.

Getting There

Head east on Interstate 90 to Exit 32, 1 mile east of North Bend, and go south on 436th Avenue SE (which becomes Cedar Falls Road SE) for about 3 miles to the Iron Horse State Park parking lot and trailhead. Elevation: 950 feet.

The Trail

Pick up the wide, obvious, and well-signed John Wayne Pioneer Trail and start walking toward Eastern Washington, where, by the shores of the Columbia River, the 100-mile rail trail eventually ends. Of course you won't be going nearly that far, only about 0.5 mile from the trailhead.

Little Si and Big Si from Cedar Butte

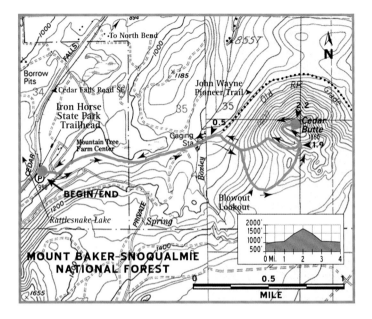

Note the "Keep Out" signs to the right, warning you to stay out of the 91,000-acre Cedar River Watershed, which the trail borders. A few years ago I was walking this trail and I had the thought: "Wow, 91,000 acres and no one's allowed in there; I bet there're critters galore around here." Just then a black bear popped out of the woods and onto the trail about 200 yards ahead of me. I immediately wished for a bag of gold and a house overlooking Haro Strait on the west side of San Juan Island in the hopes that they, too, would materialize, but alas, they never did.

Back on the trail, check out views of craggy Rattlesnake Ledge (Hike 40) to the west, and just after crossing (signed) Boxley Creek via a wood bridge, look for a small sign on the right pointing the way to Cedar Butte. Immediately, the trail climbs steeply up an old clear-cut that is quickly repairing itself, feeling more and more like forest as the years go by. At **1.2** miles, go right at an unsigned intersection (the old sign was torn down at some point). The way right leads to the Blowout, traversing a level side-hill stretch for a few hundred yards.

Just beyond where the trail resumes climbing, reach the (signed) Boxley Blowout overlook, which these days is overgrown and overlooks a lot of trees. The trail resumes climbing, enters deeper forest, and at **1.9** miles reaches a signed intersection. Remember this spot. Now you'll head up, climbing about a third of a mile to the top; on the way down, however, you'll bear right and head down.

The last stretch climbs about 300 feet in 0.3 mile, with views opening up to reveal Rattlesnake Mountain, its namesake lake, and the John Wayne Trail below. At **2.2** miles reach the top, a mini summit a shade under 2,000 feet high. Much is overgrown, but views to the north and east are grand—Mount Si and Little Si; Mailbox Peak and Mount Washington, gateway to the Central Cascades; the Snoqualmie River valley; and much more. After wowing at the views from up top, take a moment to nurture your inner Beavis and Butthead—note the survey marker at your feet and, in particular, its misspelling of the peak on which you stand: "Ceder Butt," it reads. Heh-heh, heh-heh, heh-heh. Cool.

On the way back down, for variety go right at the last intersection you reached before the summit and in about a third of a mile, reach the Boxley Blowout intersection you reached at 1.2 miles. From here return the same way you came.

Going Farther
The Cedar Butte Trail uses the same trailhead as John Wayne Pioneer Trail–Iron Horse State Park (Hike 41). ∎

43. Mailbox Peak

RATING	DISTANCE	HIKING TIME
★★★★☆	6.0 miles round-trip (old trail) 9.4 miles (new trail)	6 hours

ELEVATION GAIN	HIGH POINT	DIFFICULTY
3,900 feet	4,841 feet	◆◆◆◆◆

BEST SEASON											
Jan	Feb	Mar	Apr	May	Jun	Jul	Aug	Sep	Oct	Nov	Dec

The Hike

We now have two trails to the quirky summit of Mailbox Peak. You can kick it old school on the straight-up-the-gut route that is legendary for its steepness. Or you can use the pleasant, much longer route crafted by Mountains to Sound Greenway and the Department of Natural Resources. Either one takes you to a place with fantastic views from Mount Baker to Mount Rainier, Puget Sound, and the Olympics. And of course, there's the nominal mailbox at the summit—who knows what you'll find inside.

Getting There

Go east on Interstate 90 to Exit 34, about 3 miles east of North Bend, and turn left onto 468th Avenue SE. In about 0.75 miles, just past the East Seattle Truck Plaza, turn right onto Middle Fork Road. Follow it for about 2.2 miles to the trailhead parking lot. Note: this is a popular hike—arrive early to get a spot, or you may need to find a place to park along Middle Fork Road. Elevation: 1,020 feet.

The Trail

Heading east from North Bend, Mailbox Peak is on the left, like the westernmost bookend for Defiance Ridge, which looms high above I-90 almost all the way to Snoqualmie Pass. It's directly across from Mount Washington, the westernmost bookend on the south side of the freeway.

Leaving the parking lot, it's time to choose. Do you go straight up on the shorter old trail or take the longer, more forgiving new trail? The answer for many people is to do both—hike up the old trail and hike down the new, making this a loop. If you do, it's roughly 7.3 miles round-trip.

The Old Trail

Start climbing on a gated gravel road past a kiosk and signs for Mailbox Peak. Ignore them: that's the new trail they're talking about. Your trailhead is about **0.4** mile away on the left. Enter the forest and let the suffering begin. The route is rough, rocky, and root-strewn, going straight up the mountainside. Switchbacks? Obviously, they are for wimps.

This route is favored by climbers training for Mount Rainier. You'll see many big packs carried by burly legs struggling on the vertical assault. Your hands will come in handy as you push ever upward.

Because the trail is so rough, it braids in spots. Try your best to stay on the main trail and keep from eroding the mountain. Finally, at **2.2** miles the first views open up toward Mount Rainier and Washington, and you're reminded why you're doing this trail in the first place. Just ahead, the trail swings to the left where it joins with the new trail. Then you'll reach a boulder field and ridge for the final 500-foot push to the top at **3** miles.

Once on the summit, check out the sights: A full-on 360-degree mountains-to-sound-to-urban panorama that takes in the Olympics, downtown Seattle, Mount Rainier, and seemingly all of the North

PERMITS/CONTACT
Discover Pass required/Washington State Department of Natural Resources, South Puget Sound Region, (360) 825-1631

MAPS
USGS Chester Morse Lake; Green Trails Bandera 206, Mount Si NRCA 206S

TRAIL NOTES
Leashed dogs okay; great views; old trail is extremely steep

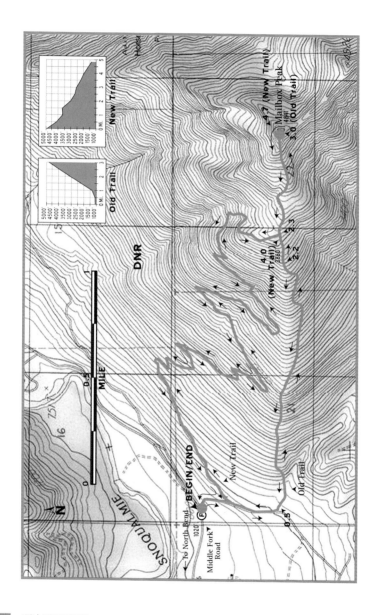

and Central Cascades. Then there's the mailbox—you never know what you'll find inside. On a recent trip, there was a bag of rice, hand sanitizer, toy cars, a candy bar, and a nearly full bottle of Jim Beam. Nearby, a flag fluttered in the breeze.

The New Trail

If the old route is best suited to mountain goats, the new route is actually a trail. One that you can actually walk on instead of stepping, sliding, grunting, and cursing as you scramble along. Starting at the kiosk about 100 yards up the gravel road from the parking lot, you'll contour east along the flank of mountain, climbing steadily into a deciduous forest. One of the benefits of this trail is that it takes you deeper into forest, crossing streams on artfully placed stepping stones, and away from the traffic noises of I-90.

At about **0.8** mile, you'll reach the first of many switchbacks and enter a mixed evergreen forest. At **1.0** mile, you'll cross a lovely stream on a fancy new bridge; give thanks for this civilized pathway and the many volunteer hours donated by Washington Trails Association that it took to build.

Your switchbacks continue through the forested slopes for about 3 miles. The hillside steepness increases as you go, but the trail grade never gets unmanageable. It averages 15 percent and only steepens when you reach the junction with the old trail. By then, you'll have views to help you on your final assault to the top.

Both trails are hikeable all year, but the steep top holds snow into late spring. Early season, an ice ax isn't a bad idea, and trekking poles will help, too.

Going Farther

The Middle Fork Snoqualmie River Trail (Hike 44) is about 9 miles up the valley. Trails for Little Si (Hike 37), Mount Si (Hike 38), and Talus Loop Trail (Hike 39) are just across the valley on Mount Si Road. ■

44. Middle Fork Snoqualmie River

RATING	DISTANCE	HIKING TIME
★ ★ ★ ☆ ☆	**6.0 miles round-trip**	**3 hours**
ELEVATION GAIN	**HIGH POINT**	**DIFFICULTY**
350 feet	**1,150 feet**	◆ ◆ ◆ ◆ ◆

BEST SEASON
Jan **Feb Mar Apr May Jun Jul Aug Sep Oct Nov** Dec

The Hike

Snow-free almost year-round, this valley walk plunges deep into the river valley and offers a range of hiking possibilities. From short, morning walks to all-day excursions, the trail, which passes through old- and second-growth forest alternately, hugs the glacier-fed river and the rocky canyon walls.

Getting There

Go east on Interstate 90 to Exit 34, about 3 miles east of North Bend, and turn left onto 468th Avenue SE. In about 0.75 mile, just past the East Seattle Truck Plaza, turn right onto Middle Fork Road, also called Forest Service Road 56. Follow it for 11.6 miles to the large parking lot on the right side of the road. (Don't worry when the road splits early on, it meets up again just ahead.) Elevation: 1,000 feet.

The Trail

Much of the scenic beauty of this forest-heavy trail is experienced right off the bat. From the trailhead, pass through dense woodland of moss- and fern-floored greenery to hemlocks so thick they appear to turn off the sun. (Sure, it's been logged before—this area has rich logging, mining, trapping, and all-around manhandling-of-nature history—but it's still impressive.)

A major landslide in 2018 closed the trail 1.1 miles from the trailhead, but forest crews were working to clear the mess and restore the trail at the time of this book's publication. For the latest conditions, contact the North Bend Ranger District (425) 888-1421.

Just ahead cross the Middle Fork Snoqualmie River via the way-cool Gateway Bridge with its stunning wood arches, and head to the left (upstream). The majestic, craggy face of Garfield Mountain across the river emerges through the trees, all 4,896 feet of it. Follow as the trail snakes its way riverside, around and through mossy boulders, massive stumps and tree trunks; slimy, slippery slugs; and plants and flowers galore—your skunk cabbage, your trillium, your salmonberry, your coltsfoot, and so on.

At about **0.5** mile the trail climbs a bit away from the river, and views of Stegosaurus Butte emerge to the right. Soon enough the trail is practically hugging the butte's rocky wall. The trail meanders on through the forest. At about **1.7** miles the trail follows an old railroad grade. In total, the trail continues about 14.3 miles (one-way) from the trailhead to Dutch Miller Gap on the other side of Snoqualmie Pass. For our day-hiking purposes, however, a good turnaround point is at about **3.0** miles, where the trail returns to the river's edge.

Note: Being as densely wooded as this trail is, it's not surprising that the potential (and likelihood) of blowdown is quite high. Thus, don't be surprised if you find yourself taking giant steps over, or even hugging and then trying to fling your body over, downed logs that have yet to be cleared. If you're concerned, call the ranger for the latest conditions before heading out.

PERMITS/CONTACT
Northwest Forest Pass required/Mount Baker–Snoqualmie National Forest,
North Bend Ranger District, (425) 888-1421

MAPS
USGS Lake Philippa; Green Trails Mount Si 174, Skykomish 175

TRAIL NOTES
Leashed dogs okay; kid-friendly; river environment; bikes okay on
odd-numbered days from June 1 to October 31

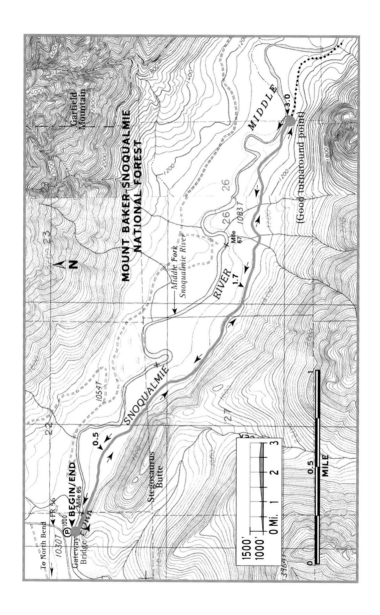

Garfield Mountain with its summit in the clouds

Going Farther

For the burly at heart (and lungs and muscles) this trail has many options. At about 5.8 miles along the Middle Fork Trail, reach the intersection with the Dingford Creek Trail, which crosses the Middle Fork Snoqualmie River and follows Dingford Creek for about 6 miles.

The Snow Lake–High Lakes end of the world can accessed from the Middle Fork Trail as well. About 2.7 miles past the Dingford Creek Trail, pick up the Rock Creek Trail on the right. It climbs 4.3 miles to Snow Lake. ■

I-90 CORRIDOR

RATING	DISTANCE	HIKING TIME
★★★☆☆	2.6 miles round-trip	2 hours
ELEVATION GAIN	**HIGH POINT**	**DIFFICULTY**
720 feet	1,000 feet	◆◇◇◇◇
BEST SEASON		
Jan Feb Mar Apr May Jun Jul Aug Sep Oct Nov Dec		

The Hike

Just 35 miles east of Seattle in Olallie State Park, the rain falls by the bucket—about 90 inches per year, or about two-and-a-half times as much as the Emerald City receives. This pleasant rain-forest walk provides a tasty appetizer, and Lower and Upper Twin Falls—one a plunger, one opting more to fan out across a rock face—provide the main course.

Getting There

Go east on Interstate 90 to Exit 34, about 3 miles east of North Bend, and turn right onto 468th Avenue SE. In 0.6 mile turn left on SE 159th Street and follow it for 0.6 mile into Olallie State Park and the road-end trailhead parking lot. Elevation: 620 feet.

The Trail

This trail starts in the Twin Falls Natural Area in Olallie State Park, a 3.5-mile-long narrow slice of natural wonder that roughly parallels I-90 between Exits 34 and 38. ("Olallie" is a Chinook word meaning "berry.") Upon entering the forest, you'll soon become acquainted with the South Fork of the Snoqualmie River. Here it's mild, just plying its way through boulders, bars, and snags, seemingly meek and mild. But, oh, hike this trail and it's quite a different beast upriver—catching about 150 feet of air at one point like some gosh-darned creek in an X Games competition. Overall, the river drops 454 feet via a series of cascades in about a mile.

Follow the trail as it parallels the river through lush, old growth that, given the 90-inch annual rainfall here, feels and looks for all the

Lower Twin Falls drops more than 150 feet

PERMITS/CONTACT
Discover Pass required/Washington State Parks, (360) 902-8844

MAPS
USGS Chester Morse Lake; Green Trails Bandera 206,
Rattlesnake Mountain 205S

TRAIL NOTES
Leashed dogs okay; kid-friendly; great waterfalls

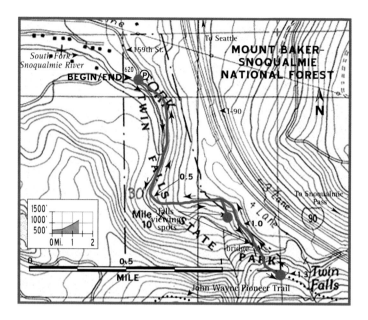

world like a rain forest. Tree trunks and boulders are cloaked in green fur and look to be warding off the cold and damp by wearing sweaters knit from various mosses and lichens.

All the precipitation that falls here sometimes leads to flooding and slides on the steep hillside. In 2006 and again in 2014, major floods damaged the hiking trails, but they have been repaired nicely.

At about **0.5** mile the trail tears itself from the river for a short stretch and climbs to a saddle, which when reached about a quarter- mile farther, reveals the first partially obstructed views of the Lower Twin Falls. They're stunning, the sound of the crashing water thrilling as all heck. Two benches are there to enjoy the long view of the falls, and it's worth pausing for a moment to soak it all in. This is just an appetizer— you'll get much closer on a viewing platform ahead.

The trail drops down a hillside among some mega-old fir trees— some up to 14 feet in diameter. At about **1.0** mile a set of wooden stairs leads down to a viewing deck with jaw-dropping, seemingly reach-out-and-touch views of the rushing, gushing, rock face–fanning Lower Twin Falls. It's front row in the great Gravity-versus-Snoqualmie River wrestling match and, even though the outcome is always the same—the South Fork takes the 150-foot fall—it is truly thrilling. The effect is that of a great fireworks display—no matter what age, we become nine-year-olds again, filled with wonder to the point of silence.

To reach the Upper Falls, climb back up the stairs and once back on the trail, go right. After climbing for a few hundred feet, round a bend and descend some steps to the neat 80-foot bridge that spans the river canyon between both the Upper and Lower Falls. Most likely, you'll find yourself leaning against the railing and staring down, mesmerized by paisley-shaped swirls and whirlpools as the rushing water churns its way past rocks and boulders and sandbars. Snags and stumps choke threads of the river, waiting for rains to send enough water blasting through the canyon so they can ride the rapids up and over the Lower Falls. During late summer, as little as 200 gallons of water per second makes its way through the river gorge. But throughout the winter and spring the flow increases until as much as 5,000 gallons per second is tumbling over the cliffs here.

Beyond the bridge, more wooden steps lead to a viewpoint at about **1.3** miles that looks head-on at the Upper Falls. The water here falls Slinky-like, from one rock tier to the next, finally plunging into a cool, deep pool at the bottom.

Going Farther

The trail continues climbing for about a half-mile, eventually hooking up with the John Wayne Pioneer Trail. It's possible to do a one-way hike via a car shuttle. Leave a second car at Olallie State Park just up the freeway. Take Exit 38 and turn right. Go 0.2 mile and turn right into the Homestead Valley Trailhead parking lot. ■

46. Weeks Falls

RATING	DISTANCE	HIKING TIME
★★☆☆☆	0.7-mile loop	30 minutes
ELEVATION GAIN	**HIGH POINT**	**DIFFICULTY**
30 feet	1,200 feet	◆◇◇◇◇

BEST SEASON
Jan **Feb Mar Apr May Jun Jul Aug Sep Oct Nov** Dec

The Hike
Quietude, solitude, an improved attitude—all are to be found on this short, gentle interpretive walk along the South Fork of the Snoqualmie through dense forest. Weeks Falls, at the end of a 100-yard barrier-free stretch, is a gurgling cascade perfect for kids and those who might have trouble getting around.

Getting There
Go east on Interstate 90 to Exit 38, about 7 miles east of North Bend, to Old Highway 10. Follow the road for 0.8 mile and turn left into the Olallie State Park parking lot. Elevation: 1,200 feet.

The Trail
Start near the oversized vehicles parking lot and follow the sound of water. That's the Snoqualmie River making a dash for the Sound. It's mossy and ferny and densely wooded and feels like a rain forest in here, and no wonder. This is the east end of Olallie State Park, where

PERMITS/CONTACT
Discover Pass required/Washington State Parks, (360) 902-8844

MAPS
USGS Chester Morse Lake; Green Trails Mount Si NRCA 206S

TRAIL NOTES
Leashed dogs okay; kid-friendly; paved section near the falls is barrier-free

A small hydroelectric plant is powered by Weeks Falls

the precip falls at two-and-a-half times the rate that it does in Seattle, fewer than 40 miles away.

Follow the wide, gravel trail east as it parallels the river, offering access points here and there so you can watch the river do its rock-hopping, boulder-squeezing thing, and also contemplate the peaceful spots where the water pools. Back on the trail, check out the interpretive signs that tell the tale of how this trail follows the route of a former puncheon road that was built in the 1890s by prospectors making their way for the mountain and the gold they believed was in them thar hills. When the first highway across Snoqualmie Pass was built in 1915, the puncheon road was abandoned, but to this day many of the puncheons—logs split in half on which travelers rode—can still be found in the ground.

At about **0.3** mile, reach a gate and just beyond, a small parking lot. The falls and a viewing area are about 100 yards ahead, at the end of a paved, barrier-free stretch. The falls, which power a small hydroelectric plant, cascade about 30 or 40 feet. They're not huge,

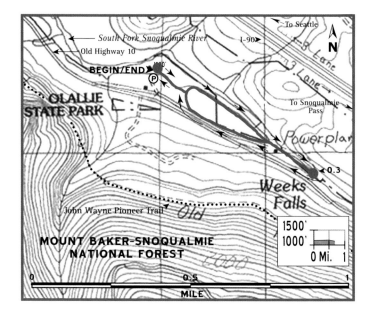

but impressive nonetheless, especially after times of heavy rainfall or snowmelt.

The trail is basically a figure-eight loop, so when it's time to head back, follow the other part of the loop. Closer to the parking lot, take note of the rock climbers spidering their way up the rock cliffs to the left (south; the side opposite the river).

Going Farther

The John Wayne Pioneer Trail–Iron Horse State Park (Hike 41) passes right by Olallie State Park. ∎

47. Dirty Harry's Balcony

RATING	DISTANCE	HIKING TIME
★★★☆☆	5.0 miles round-trip	3 hours

ELEVATION GAIN	HIGH POINT	DIFFICULTY
1,300 feet	2,600 feet	◆◆◆◇◇

BEST SEASON
Jan Feb **Mar Apr May Jun Jul Aug Sep Oct Nov** Dec

The Hike
You have to wonder what "Dirty" Harry Gault would think of a hike named in his honor. After all, Gault is infamous for his zealous logging practices—and his ability to build landscape-scarring roads—in these mountains. These days, Harry's old logging roads are healing, and this hike crosses them in places to reach a terrific viewpoint overlooking the South Fork of the Snoqualmie River and Interstate 90 corridor. Views of McClellan Butte and Defiance Ridge dominate.

Getting There
Go east on Interstate 90 to Exit 38, about 7 miles east of North Bend, and turn right (south) onto Old Highway 10, following the signs for Olallie State Park and State Fire Training Academy. Cross under the freeway at 1.9 miles and just ahead, park at the Far Side Trailhead for Olallie State Park. (Note: The old trailhead for this hike used to be inside the Fire Training Academy, but that access is no longer allowed.

PERMITS/CONTACT
Discover Pass required/Department of Natural Resources South Puget Sound Region (360) 825-1631

MAPS
USGS Chester Morse Lake, Bandera; Green Trails Mount Si/Snoqualmie Pass Gateway 207S

TRAIL NOTES
Leashed dogs okay; unusual views

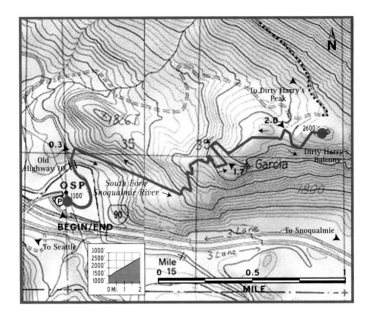

Hikers must now park before entering the academy.) Elevation: 1,300 feet.

The Trail

Thanks to the State Department of Natural Resources, Mountains to Sound Greenway Trust, and Washington Trails Association, a new trail was added to Dirty Harry's Balcony in 2017. Start at the Far Side trailhead and walk about 200 yards through the trees, where you'll hit the roadway into the fire academy. Take a left and cross the South Fork of the Snoqualmie River on a one-lane bridge. The rushing water here feeds Weeks Falls (Hike 46) and Twin Falls (Hike 45) lower down.

Just across the bridge at **0.3 mile**, the trail continues on the right. If you've passed the guardrail, you've gone too far. Climb through deep forest along the South Fork of the Snoqualmie on the new Birdhouse Trail. Passing boulders, reach a steep set of switchbacks and pass spur trails to the right. Stay left as you climb through forest and up the

Dirty Harry's Balcony is high above the hustle and bustle

ridgeline. At 1.7 miles, reach the Birdhouse on a tree overlooking the I-90 Corridor. This is a great place for lunch and a turnaround.

Back on the trail, climb higher along the ridge. At 2.0 miles, you'll reach a fork marked by a cairn on a large boulder. The left fork goes to Dirty Harry's Peak; the right goes to the Balcony.

Hang a right and within about 100 yards, take another right at another fork. Within minutes, you'll reach your balcony seat.

Hiking guidebook author Harvey Manning dubbed this area Dirty Harry's Peak after gazing upon the destruction reaped by the logger's well-used chainsaw in the 1960s. Evidence of the clear-cuts remains, but Mother Nature is doing her best to heal the damage.

Views here are outstanding—McClellan Peak, Defiance Ridge, Snoqualmie Pass, and, almost directly overhead, Dirty Harry's Peak. Craggy outcrops offer the perfect place to relax as busy people careen down the freeway below. Luckily, you're not one of them.

Going Farther

Peak-baggers may follow the route to the top of Dirty Harry's Peak another 4 miles and 2,100 vertical feet. ∎

48. McClellan Butte

RATING	DISTANCE	HIKING TIME
★★★★☆	9.2 miles round-trip	6 hours
ELEVATION GAIN	HIGH POINT	DIFFICULTY
3,750 feet	5,162 feet	◆◆◆◆◇

BEST SEASON
Jan Feb Mar Apr May Jun **Jul Aug Sep Oct** Nov Dec

The Hike

Ready. Set. Climb! That's the theme of this trail to the top of one of the more prominent peaks looming over Interstate 90 on the way to Snoqualmie Pass. You get up high, but because the views from the top are slightly obstructed—unless, that is, you partake of the potentially dangerous rock scramble to the true summit—you don't get the crowds here that you do on Granite Mountain across the valley.

Getting There

Head east on Interstate 90 to Exit 42, about 11.0 miles east of North Bend, and turn right onto gravel West Tinkham Road. Continue for about 0.3 mile, then turn right onto gravel Forest Road 5500-101. The road-end trailhead is about 0.2 mile ahead. Elevation: 1,580 feet.

Views east toward Snoqualmie Pass

The Trail

First off, the first mile of this trail isn't really indicative of what you're in for. From the trailhead, climb gradually through forest, cross under some power lines, and at about **0.6** mile, reach the John Wayne Pioneer Trail, the 100-mile rail trail that stretches from the Columbia River in Eastern Washington to North Bend. (It's quite obvious and is *not* the overgrown gravel road you cross a couple hundred yards before the Iron Horse.) Go right and follow the level trail for a little less than a half-mile to the signed McClellan Butte trailhead on your left.

PERMITS/CONTACT
Discover Pass required/Department of Natural Resources, South Puget Sound Region, (360) 825-1631

MAPS
USGS Chester Morse Lake, Bandera; Green Trails Mount Si/Snoqualmie Pass Gateway 207S

TRAIL NOTES
Leashed dogs okay; unusual views

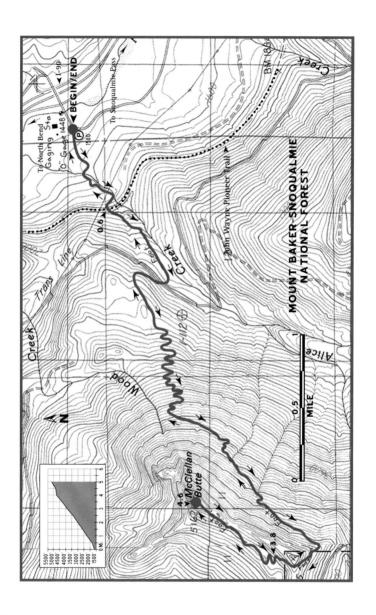

Say goodbye to the phrase "level trail" and begin climbing in earnest pretty much immediately. The next 3.6 miles climb about 3,300 feet and most of that is under forest cover, so hopefully you're hiking with someone whose conversation you find fascinating. Luckily, from time to time, views do open up revealing awesome vistas toward the mountains crowding Snoqualmie Pass, south toward Mount Rainier, and down to Chester Morse Lake, the reservoir that provides 70 percent of Seattle's water supply. The trail crosses a number of exposed gullies that can hang onto snow well into the hiking season, making for early-season avalanche danger and, later, slippery and potentially dangerous snow crossings. Before heading out, check with the ranger for the latest conditions.

At about **3.8** miles the trail swings around to the west side of the mountain, offering at first stunning views of Rainier and then alarming ones at the clear-cuts on neighboring Mount Washington. Heading north now, the trail drops about 150 feet to a small tarn in a meadowy area. Resume climbing and at **4.6** miles the trail ends at what feels like the back of the butte. The views are grand, all 270-degrees of them, from mountains far beyond Snoqualmie Pass to the east and the Snoqualmie Valley, North Bend, Puget Sound, and the Olympics to the west. Views spread out to the south, too, but to the north is nothing but McClellan's big butte.

Experienced climbers often scramble to the top of the butte (about another 100 feet), but it is by no means a gimme. A fall would be fatal, no ifs, ands, or buts about it. McClellan Butte is named for George McClellan, who in the decade before he'd gain fame as one of the best-known Civil War generals, scouted this area for a possible trans-Cascade railroad route.

Going Farther
Camping is available at Tinkham Campground, about 1 mile east of the trailhead off Tinkham Road. ◼

49. Ira Spring Trail

RATING	DISTANCE	HIKING TIME
★★★★★	7.0 miles round-trip	5 hours

ELEVATION GAIN	HIGH POINT	DIFFICULTY
3,041 feet	5,241 feet	◆◆◆◆

BEST SEASON
Jan Feb Mar Apr **May Jun Jul Aug Sep Oct** Nov Dec

The Hike

Improvements made last decade on the former Mason Lake Trail have made this a pretty straightforward ascent to one of the many peaks looming high on Interstate 90's north flank. Views are many and on summer weekends so are the crowds, although they thin out markedly on the last mile—a 1,000-foot push to the top. When the trail was improved, it was renamed in memory of Ira Spring, the Northwest hiking author, photographer, and trails advocate who died in 2003.

Getting There

Head east on Interstate 90 to Exit 45, about 14 miles east of North Bend. Go north across the freeway and just ahead turn left onto Forest Service Road 9030. In about 0.5 mile the road turns to gravel; stay left at the fork onto Forest Road 9031 and follow it another 3.5 miles to the road-end trailhead. Elevation 2,200 feet.

PERMITS/CONTACT
Northwest Forest Pass required/Mount Baker–Snoqualmie National Forest, North Bend Ranger District, (425) 888-1421

MAPS
USGS Bandera; Green Trails Bandera 206, Snoqualmie Pass Gateway 207S

TRAIL NOTES
Leashed dogs okay; great views

Bandera Mountain hikers leave the city behind

The Trail

Formerly an old anglers' route that scrambled up one boulder field after another in a hurry to get to Mason Lake, the trail's 2003 make-over has transformed it largely into a way-wide trail following an old roadbed. It takes its time, climbing gradually across Bandera Mountain's southern flank but all the while offering views south to McClellan Butte, deep down into the I-90 corridor, and eventually to Mount Rainier, which rises high to dominate the sky as only Rainier can.

At about **1.0** mile the grade increases markedly as you climb in and out of forest. However, the trees are never so dense that you're long without mountain views. Continue climbing and after leaving the trees, reach an signed intersection at about **2.5** miles with the Mason Lake–Mount Defiance Trail (Hike 50). To go left is to eventually drop a couple hundred feet into the Mason Lake (and Little Mason Lake and Lake Kulla Kulla) basin.

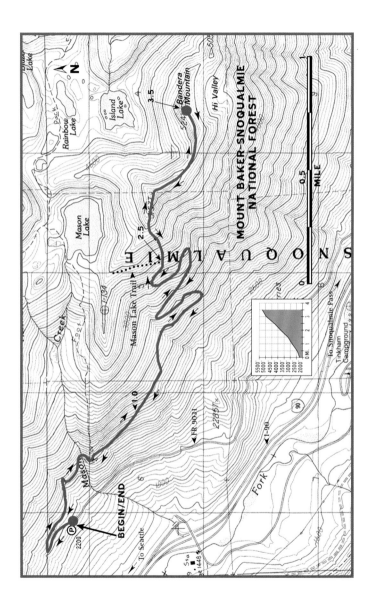

Go right at the junction and watch that your knees don't smack your chin making the big steps required for the final thousand-foot-push, seemingly straight up to the top of Bandera Mountain. Most of the final climb is in the open with wildflowers and spectacular views accompanying you the whole way. A couple stretches through rock garden with granite flakes the size of car doors require hands as well as feet. But the 360-degree views from the rocky top are more than worth whatever hardship it takes to get you here. Count the volcanoes—Baker to Glacier Peak to Rainier to Adams—and views west to Seattle, Puget Sound, and the Olympics. Hike the summit ridge for as far as you're comfortable or the views seem worth it. Trees obstruct the view from the actual highest point. ■

50. Mason Lake–Mount Defiance

RATING	DISTANCE	HIKING TIME
★★★★★	7.0 miles round-trip for the lake; 10.0 miles round-trip for Mount Defiance	4 hours for the lake; 6 hours for Mount Defiance
ELEVATION GAIN	HIGH POINT	DIFFICULTY
2,400 feet; 3,750 feet	5,584 feet	◆◆◆◆
BEST SEASON		
Jan Feb Mar Apr May Jun Jul Aug Sep Oct Nov Dec		

The Hike
Rerouted in 2003, this trail leads to a land of peaceful alpine lakes and a tall peak looming high on Interstate 90's north side. This approach to Mason Lake is more tame and gets rid of the boulder field crossing.

Getting There
Head east on I-90 to Exit 45, about 14 miles east of North Bend. Go north across the freeway and just ahead turn left onto Forest Service

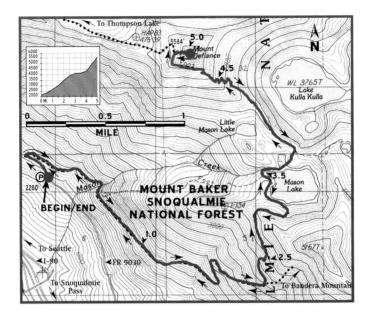

Road 9030. In about 0.5 mile the road turns to gravel; stay left at the fork onto Forest Road 9031 and follow it another 3.5 miles to the road-end trailhead. Elevation: 2,200 feet.

The Trail

Formerly an old anglers' route that scrambled up one boulder field after another in a hurry to get to Mason Lake, the trail's 2003 makeover has transformed its lower reaches into a wide trail that follows an old roadbed. It takes its time, climbing gradually across Bandera Mountain's southern flank while offering views south to McClellan Butte, the I-90 corridor and Snoqualmie River valley, and eventually Mount Rainier.

At about **1.0** mile the grade increases markedly as you climb in and out of forest. Continue climbing and after leaving the trees, reach a signed intersection at about **2.5** miles with the Ira Spring Trail (Hike 49) that leads to the summit of Bandera Mountain. For Mason Lake

Partially snow-covered Mount Defiance in the distance

and Mount Defiance go left, and after traversing a slope for a short stretch—Mount Defiance is prominent in the near distance; make note of the snow level there—enter the Alpine Lakes Wilderness and drop in to the densely wooded Mason Lake basin.

At **3.5** miles reach the lake. Continue around to the left of the lake, crossing Mason Creek at the mouth to the north side of the lake. Rising high to the southeast is Bandera Mountain, blocking the sun if you're here on a morning visit. Enjoy a snack and while you do, consider your options—doing the lakeside hang-out thing, possibly an exploratory visit to Little Mason Lake, or doing the climbing thing to 5,584-foot Mount Defiance and its spectacular vista.

PERMITS/CONTACT
Northwest Forest Pass required/Mount Baker–Snoqualmie National Forest, North Bend Ranger District, (425) 888-1421

MAPS
USGS Bandera; Green Trails Bandera 206, Snoqualmie Pass Gateway 207S

TRAIL NOTES
Leashed dogs okay; kid-friendly—to Mason Lake; great views; peaceful alpine lakes

If it's early in the season and you're opting for Defiance, hopefully you made note where the snow level is as you traversed the open hillside before entering the Mason Lake basin. The snow clears earlier lower down and although the trail near the lake can be passable, higher on the mountain the lingering snow can make for some slow and possibly dangerous going.

On the north side of the lake, hike for a few hundred yards to a signed intersection. Go left, following the arrow that points to Mount Defiance. It's a mountaintop you're heading for, so the trail gains elevation in a hurry as it follows the ridge. You'll likely be huffin' and puffin'. That's Lake Kulla Kulla down and to your right, visible at times through the trees. At **4.5** miles reach a broad, open slope, which in July is often ablaze with wildflowers. Views are gi-normous, too—Rainier, the Snoqualmie River valley, and, unfortunately, the multiple clear-cuts on the south side of the freeway.

Follow the trail to the far (west) end of the open slope and go right (that is, up) on the steep, primitive route that leads the last few hundred yards to the summit at **5.0** miles. Twirl around as you take in the 360-mountain views that seem to encompass all of Western Washington, from Mounts Baker to Rainier, from the Olympics to the Stuart Range. Bandera Mountain is the 5,200-foot nubbin in the foreground to the east, surrounded by a family of lakes.

Going Farther

The Ira Spring Trail (Hike 49) uses the same trailhead and follows the same trail for the first 2.5 miles. The Mount Defiance Trail continues for about 2 more miles past Mount Defiance to Thompson Lake. The little-used trail loses about 1,500 feet of elevation on the way to the lake. Camping is available at Tinkham Campground, at Exit 42 off I-90. ∎

51. Talapus–Olallie Lakes

RATING	DISTANCE	HIKING TIME
★★★☆☆	4.0 miles round-trip for Talapus Lake; 6.0 miles round-trip for Olallie Lake	2 hours for Talapus Lake; 3 hours for Olallie Lake

ELEVATION GAIN	HIGH POINT	DIFFICULTY
800 feet; 1,300 feet	3,750 feet	◆◆◇◇◇

BEST SEASON
Jan Feb Mar Apr May Jun **Jul Aug Sep Oct** Nov Dec

The Hike

This pair of easily reached alpine lakes can be quiet and contemplative and offer scads of staring-into-the-water time. During weekdays, that is. On summer weekends, however, you won't be lonely up here. That said, it's still a great place for young families to get that first backpacking or day-hiking trip under their belt.

Getting There

Head east on Interstate 90 to Exit 45, about 14.0 miles east of North Bend, and head north across the freeway. Turn left onto Forest Road 9030 and in just under 1 mile, turn right and continue on FR 9030 for 2.4 miles to the road-end trailhead parking lot. Elevation: 2,600 feet.

PERMITS/CONTACT

Northwest Forest Pass required/Mount Baker–Snoqualmie National Forest, North Bend Ranger District, (425) 888-1421

MAPS

USGS Bandera; Green Trails Bandera 206, Snoqualmie Pass Gateway 207S

TRAIL NOTES

Leashed dogs okay; kid-friendly; great lakeside views

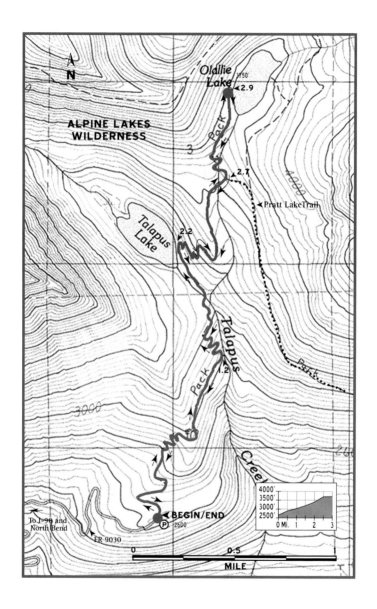

N

Olallie
Lake
3750'
◄2.9

ALPINE LAKES
WILDERNESS

3

◄2.7

►Pratt Lake Trail

Talapus
Lake
2.2

Talapus

Pack

1.2

3000

Pack

Creek

2600'

BEGIN/END
Ⓟ 2600'

To I-90 and
North Bend

FR 9030

4000'
3500'
3000'
2500'
0 Mi. 1   2   3

0   0.5   1
MILE

In the summer, the lakes offer a refreshing break from hiking

The Trail

Start out on a wide former logging road, entering the forest via a gentle grade that's easy on the quads and calves. In fall watch your head as a trailhead sign often warns of butterfingered squirrels who often drop pine cones on hikers' noggins. At times the trail alternates between boardwalk and rough, root-strewn stretches, and at about **1.2** miles it meets up with Talapus Creek, tumbling over rocks down the hillside, for the first time.

The trail switchbacks several times, approaching then leaving the creek each time, and in about a half-mile, a sign informs you that you've just entered the Alpine Lakes Wilderness. Just ahead, go right at a fork—following the "Main Trail" sign—and after crossing a damp, marshy area via boardwalk and log bridge, go left at another fork. Drop down for a short stretch and at **2.0** miles reach Talapus Lake. Relax and take a load off.

For Olallie Lake, get back on the main trail and although various exploratory spurs lead off in seemingly all directions, look for the "Olallie Lake" sign nailed high on a tree. The trail climbs steeply— much more steeply than the trail to Talapus Lake—and is a bit rocky at times. At about **2.7** miles go left at the intersection with the Pratt Lake Trail, and in about a quarter-mile, reach Olallie Lake. Because it's a mile farther and requires a little more climbing to get to, Olallie Lake offers a better chance of seclusion than Talapus.

Return the same way.

Going Farther

The Pratt Lake Trail can be accessed via a spur trail just before reaching Olallie Lake. Camping is available at the Denny Creek Campground, about 9 miles east of the trailhead on FR 58. ■

52. Granite Mountain

RATING	DISTANCE	HIKING TIME
★★★★★	8.6 miles round-trip	6 hours
ELEVATION GAIN	HIGH POINT	DIFFICULTY
3,800 feet	5,629 feet	◆◆◆◆◆
BEST SEASON		
Jan Feb Mar Apr May Jun **Jul Aug Sep Oct** Nov Dec		

The Hike

Here's a trail that's got it goin' on but makes you work for it. It's steep as heck, and not exactly baby-butt smooth either, but once you break out of the trees, you're in hills-are-alive-with-the-*Sound of Music* land. The mountain views from the historic, still-in-use lookout on top are, in a word, volcano-riffic—Mount Baker and Glacier Peak to the north, Mounts Rainier and Adams to the south. Wildflowers galore abound, too.

Getting There

Head east on Interstate 90 to Exit 47, about 16 miles east of North Bend, and head north. About 0.1 mile farther take a left. The trailhead parking lot is 0.4 mile ahead. Elevation: 1,800 feet.

Mount Rainier and the active lookout atop Granite Mountain

The Trail

Driving I-90 east, you can see your objective—the lookout, a square box perched atop a high, rocky bump—and a couple things strike you. One, it's way the heck up there and, two, the upper 2,500 feet or so of the south-facing mountain are completely in the open. That means spectacular views that'll take your mind off the hellaciously steep grade—about 1,000 feet per mile—wildflowers like crazy, and,

PERMITS/CONTACT
Northwest Forest Pass required/Mount Baker–Snoqualmie National Forest, North Bend Ranger District, (425) 888-1421

MAPS
USGS Snoqualmie Pass; Green Trails Snoqualmie Pass 207, Snoqualmie Pass Gateway 207S

TRAIL NOTES
Leashed dogs okay; great views; historic working lookout

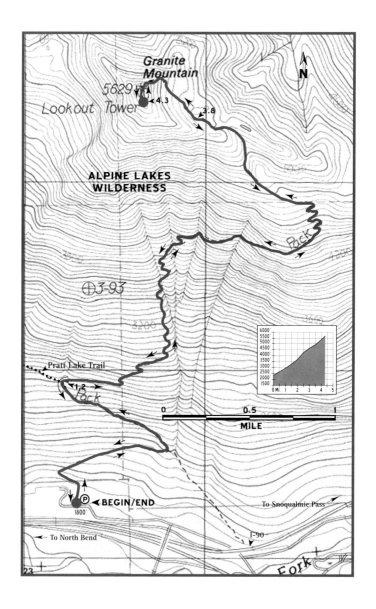

Granite
Mountain
5629'
Lookout Tower ◄4.3
3.8►

ALPINE LAKES
WILDERNESS

⊕3-93

Pack

Pratt Lake Trail
1.2►
Pack

0   0.5   1
MILE

6000'
5500'
5000'
4500'
4000'
3500'
3000'
2500'
2000'
1500'
0 Mi. 1 2 3 4 5

P ◄BEGIN/END
1800'

To Snoqualmic Pass

◄ To North Bend

I-90

Fork

N

23

on hot August afternoons, blowtorch-type heat. There's no water, so bring plenty to drink.

After filling out an Alpine Lakes Wilderness permit (free) at the trailhead, head into the forest and start climbing via a rocky, rooty, very high-use trail. For the first mile or so, Granite Mountain and Pratt Lake share the same trail, but at **1.2** miles, a signed intersection points you to the right and the Granite Mountain Lookout. The trail takes a turn for the really steep and really rocky almost immediately. The switchbacking grade is so relentless that anytime it even approaches a level stretch (which it rarely does), you feel like someone is pushing you down a hill. At about **2.0** miles the trail climbs along the edge of an avalanche chute, which can be rocky and early in the season still choked with snow. Views open up to the east and soon enough you'll find yourself climbing and traversing that giant open meadow.

Early in the season, crossing the avalanche-prone gully to that meadow can be potentially dangerous. Contact the ranger ahead of time for the latest avalanche conditions. Once out of the forest, bask in the views and, in mid- to late summer, the huckleberries and wildflowers. The higher you climb, the more the mountain views open up, allowing for that "sea of peaks" sensation. Just don't look down. You can see the freeway and, worse, hear it. Pretend it's just the ocean breeze.

At about **3.8** miles reach a flattish rock garden just below the final push to the top. Whistle back at the cheeky marmots that have no doubt been whistling at you. Snow lingers here and, early in the season, hikers often scramble along the ridge through the obvious boulder field. If conditions allow, be sure to stay on the trail and not step on vegetation, which, up this high, has a short growing season.

At **4.3** miles reach the lookout, say hi to the ranger, and do a Mary Tyler Moore spin to take in all the views. There are more than 47,000 feet worth of volcanoes and countless fewer peaks, crags, bumps, river drainages, lakes, and forests on all sides. Crystal and Tuscohatchie lakes are the ones close by to the north; to the southeast check out huge Keechelus Lake. As for the lookout itself, it's the only working lookout in the North Bend district. It was first built here in the 1920s and replaced in 1955. (Walk about 50 yards north and you can still see the obvious site of the old lookout.)

Return the same way.

Going Farther
This is also the trailhead for the Pratt Lake Trail. Camping is available at the Denny Creek Campground, about 3 miles east of the trailhead on Forest Road 58. ∎

53. Asahel Curtis Nature Trail

RATING	DISTANCE	HIKING TIME
★★★	0.75-mile loop	30 minutes
ELEVATION GAIN	**HIGH POINT**	**DIFFICULTY**
120 feet	1,980 feet	◆

BEST SEASON
Jan Feb **Mar Apr May Jun Jul Aug Sep Oct Nov** Dec

The Hike
Named for the noted outdoor photographer and Mount Rainier climbing guide, this short, pleasant loop passes through one of the Snoqualmie Valley's last remaining stands of old-growth forest. For those learning their trees, identifying signs point out which is a Douglas fir, which is a western red cedar, which is a mountain hemlock, and so on.

Getting There
Head east on Interstate 90 to Exit 47, about 16 miles east of North Bend, and turn right. Just ahead, turn left on Asahel Curtis Road (Forest Road 55). The trailhead parking lot is 0.3 mile ahead on your right. This is also the trailhead for Annette Lake (Hike 54). Elevation: 1,900 feet.

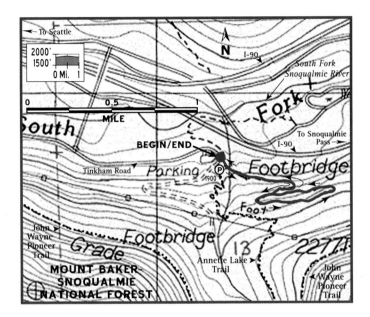

The Trail

From the parking lot, follow signs for the nature trail and soon cross Humpback Creek—for the first of several times—via a spiffy wood bridge. You can't help but be awed by the greenery that surrounds you on all sides—massive old-growth trees above (no wonder the

PERMITS/CONTACT
Northwest Forest Pass required/Mount Baker–Snoqualmie National Forest,
North Bend Ranger District, (425) 888-1421

MAPS
USGS Snoqualmie Pass; Green Trails Snoqualmie Pass 207, Snoqualmie Pass
Gateway 207S

TRAIL NOTES
Leashed dogs okay; kid-friendly; old-growth forest

Cedar limb akimbo on the Asahel Curtis Nature Trail

sun seems to have disappeared), and more mosses, ferns, orchids, and wildflowers than you can shake a stick at below. This is a great one to show out-of-towners that all that rain adds up to more than an inflated suicide rate. Massive four-foot-wide tree trunks invite you and a couple mates to do that link-hands-around-the-base-of-the-tree thing.

A few hundred yards in, check out the cool wood bench built into a couple of massive boulders. Just ahead, again follow the signs for the nature trail (you're also given the option of heading to Annette Lake). Listen for the konk-konk-konk of pileated woodpeckers working up an Excedrin headache; you might find yourself having to cover your head from the falling bark. (It's worse than their bite.) At about **1.0** mile close the loop and return to the bridge you crossed near the trailhead.

Although the trail is easy and a great one for kids, unfortunately the many rocks and roots lying in its path probably make the trail impassable for a wheelchair. Also, be aware that the cedar planks that make up part of the trail can be slippery when wet.

Going Farther

The Annette Lake Trail is accessed at the same parking lot. Camping is available at the Denny Creek Campground, about 3.0 miles east of the trailhead on Forest Road 58. ■

54. Annette Lake

RATING	DISTANCE	HIKING TIME
★★★★☆	7.8 miles round-trip	4 hours

ELEVATION GAIN	HIGH POINT	DIFFICULTY
1,900 feet	3,600 feet	◆◆◆◇◇

BEST SEASON
Jan Feb Mar Apr **May Jun Jul Aug Sep Oct Nov** Dec

The Hike

Yes, it tends to be crowded, but why wouldn't it be? It offers easy access, and it's not-too-difficult, but also not-so-tame that you're left wondering, "All right, what now for a little exercise?" There is also the cool forest and, of course, the namesake lake, a true stunner set against peaks rising a couple thousand feet. Go during the week or pack your snowshoes and go early in the year.

Getting There

Head east on Interstate 90 to Exit 47, about 16 miles east of North Bend, and turn right. Just ahead, turn left on Asahel Curtis Road (Forest Road 55). The trailhead parking lot is 0.3 mile ahead on your right. This is also the trailhead for the Asahel Curtis Nature Trail (Hike 53). Elevation: 1,900 feet.

PERMITS/CONTACT
Northwest Forest Pass required/Mount Baker–Snoqualmie National Forest, North Bend Ranger District, (425) 888-1421

MAPS
USGS Lost Lake; Green Trails Snoqualmie Pass 207, Snoqualmie Pass Gateway 207S

TRAIL NOTES
Leashed dogs okay; kid-friendly; alpine lake heaven; horses and bikes okay—for the first 0.7 mile to the John Wayne Pioneer Trail

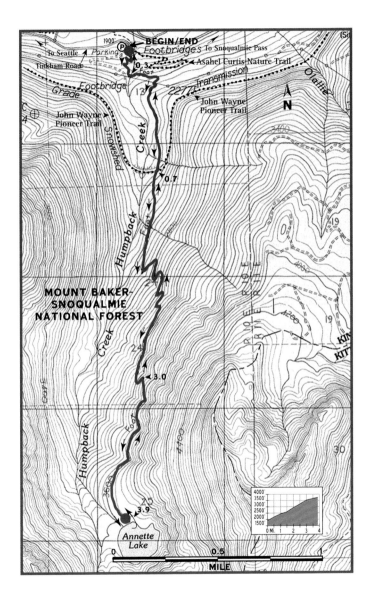

1900

Ⓟ

BEGIN/END

Footbridges To Snoqualmie Pass

To Seattle ↗ Parking

Tinkham Road

0.3

Footbridge

Grade

C 4 ⊕

John Wayne
Pioneer Trail

Snowshed

Creek

Humpback

Foot

Asahel Curtis Nature Trail

Transmission

2277

John Wayne
Pioneer Trail

N

3400

0.7

19

MOUNT BAKER-
SNOQUALMIE
NATIONAL FOREST

Creek

Gore

Humpback

Foot

3600

4800

3.0

4100

3.9

Annette
Lake

25

(St

Olallie

KIN

KIT

19

30

4000'
3500'
3000'
2500'
2000'
1500'

0 Mi. 1 2 3 4

0

0.5

1

MILE

ANNETTE LAKE | 213

An early season visit to Annette Lake

The Trail

Find the trail to the left side of the large trailhead parking lot. Following the Annette Lake sign, cross under a forest road gate, and just after, find the trail on the left as it enters the forest. After climbing for a few hundred yards, cross the Humpback Creek Bridge over the oft-raging creek of the same name. Note that the air feels cooler here by fifteen degrees.

Resume climbing through a former clear-cut via a many-rooted trail, the sounds of the freeway gradually diminishing, and at about **0.3** mile cross an old logging road which is *not* the John Wayne Pioneer Trail (Hike 41). That comes at **0.7** mile; it's a veritable freeway with signs detailing distances to its many access points. (You're 1.6 miles from the west side of the Snoqualmie Tunnel.) Once across, begin climbing steeply up through the old-growth forest on the north and west side of Silver Peak.

Several switchbacks are in your future, as are a number of scree slopes and rushing creeks that can be tricky. Occasional views of Humpback Mountain poke their way through the trees from time to time. The trail's relatively low elevation might make you think it will be clear of snow while higher routes are still buried, but you'll hit a number of avalanche chutes. An ice ax comes in handy in the early season.

At about **3.0** miles the climbing stops and it's a mostly level last mile through pleasant forest to the lake. The stunning alpine jewel is rimmed by walls of forest and rock and a triumvirate of peaks—Silver and Abiel peaks, and Humpback Mountain—loom high overhead as if looking down to check on their little Annette. Explore along the lake to the right.

Going Farther

Camping is available at the Denny Creek Campground, also off Exit 47, about 3 miles east of the trailhead. ■

55. Denny Creek–Melakwa Lake

RATING	DISTANCE	HIKING TIME
★★★★☆	9.0 miles round-trip	5 hours

ELEVATION GAIN	HIGH POINT	DIFFICULTY
2,300 feet	4,650 feet	◆◆◇◇◇

BEST SEASON
Jan Feb Mar Apr May Jun **Jul Aug Sep Oct** Nov Dec

The Hike

Plunging waterfalls, pristine alpine lakes topped by sky-scratching craggy peaks, not to mention a saunter through dense, contemplative forests—that's all on the agenda for this trail following Denny Creek to Melakwa Lake. If it's hot and you don't want to go all the way to the lake to cool off, Denny Creek's natural water slide about a mile up the trail is the perfect place to get soaked or watch others do so.

Getting There

Head east on Interstate 90 to Exit 47, about 16 miles east of North Bend, and head north. About 0.1 mile farther, turn right at the T intersection. In about 0.25 mile, turn left onto Forest Road 58 (Denny Creek Road) and follow it for about 2.5 miles to just past the Denny Creek Campground. Take a left on a road that soon crosses the river and follow it for about 0.25 mile to the Denny Creek trailhead at the end of the road. Elevation: 2,300 feet.

The Trail

From the parking lot begin a gradual climb through cool forest on a wide, well-maintained trail. At **0.3** mile cross Denny Creek (not for the last time) via a narrow bridge. Just across, the trail becomes more rocky and root-strewn. Soon hear, then see, I-90 far overhead above the treetops. Yes, I-90, a highway in the sky.

At **1.1** miles recross Denny Creek, admiring the wide, flat rocks scoured smooth by the water. The exposed slabs of bedrock make a natural water slide and water play area and, as such, draw folks seemingly by the thousands. Families with small kids might want to make this their destination and turnaround point, while others might want to save it for a reward at the end of the day. (And still others might want to avoid it altogether.)

Across the creek the trail starts climbing with meaning. In about a half-mile, leave the forest and reach an open meadow where you're suddenly surrounded on all sides by towering peaks—Low Mountain,

PERMITS/CONTACT
Northwest Forest Pass required/Mount Baker–Snoqualmie National Forest, North Bend Ranger District, (425) 888-1421

MAPS
USGS Snoqualmie Pass; Green Trails Snoqualmie Pass 207, Snoqualmie Pass Gateway 207S

TRAIL NOTES
Leashed dogs okay; kid-friendly—for first mile or so; great waterfalls and lakes

A boardwalk winds through the damp, dense forest

which doesn't appear that low, Denny Mountain, the Tooth, and others. At about **1.8** miles stop to gawk at plunging Keekwulee Falls, a 70-foot natural spigot plunging a few hundred yards to the right. Over the next 2 miles, the route offers a fairly consistent theme. It's called climbing. Cross open rocky stretches, enter forest, exit forest, cross open rocky stretches, and so on—all while getting farther and farther

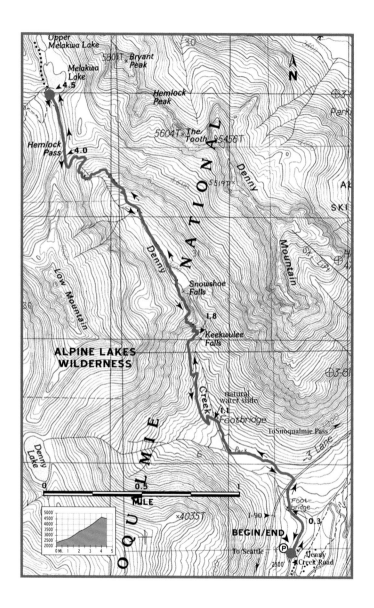

Upper
Melakwa Lake
5601T × Bryant
Peak

Melakwa
Lake
▲4.5

Hemlock
Peak

Hemlock
Pass ▲4.0

5604T × The
Tooth ×5456T

Denny

NATIONAL

Low Mountain

Denny

Snowshoe
Falls

1.8

Keekwulee
Falls

ALPINE LAKES
WILDERNESS

Creek

Mountain

SKI

natural
water slide
1.1
Footbridge

ToSnoqualmie Pass

Denny
Lake

Foot
bridge

0   0.5   1

MILE

×4035T

O   Q   U   A   L   M   I   E

5000'
4500'
4000'
3500'
3000'
2500'
2000'
0 Mi. 1 2 3 4 5

I-90 ►

Foot
bridge

0.3

BEGIN/END

To Seattle

2300'

Denny
Creek Road

N

from the center of the earth. But it's all good as you're buoyed—fairly floating on air—by the super views.

At **4.0** miles reach Hemlock Pass, at 4,600 feet, the literal high point of the trail. Almost immediately, drop quickly into the Melakwa Lake Basin. Reach the lake at **4.5** miles. It's a gem, this lake, surrounded on three sides by peaks of the 5,000- and 6,000-foot variety. From Kaleetan at the north to Chair and Bryant and the Tooth, they're all large and in charge. For a bit of exploration, continue along the left side of the lake for a few hundred yards to Upper Melakwa Lake.

Going Farther

Just before Melakwa Lake, a trail to the left leads about 3.5 miles to Pratt Lake and the Pratt Lake Trail. With two cars, the Denny Creek–Melakwa Lake Trail and the Pratt Lake Trail can be combined to make a loop hike nearly 14 miles long. Camping, full restrooms, and water are available at Denny Creek Campground near the trailhead. ■

56. Franklin Falls–Wagon Road Loop

RATING	DISTANCE	HIKING TIME
★★★☆☆	**2.0 miles round-trip**	**1 hour**

ELEVATION GAIN	HIGH POINT	DIFFICULTY
200 feet	**2,600 feet**	◆ ◇ ◇ ◇

BEST SEASON
Jan Feb Mar **Apr May Jun Jul Aug Sep Oct** Nov Dec

The Hike

Want an unobstructed view of a 75-foot horsetail of water plunging over a cliff? Then this easy stroll through old-growth forest to the base of Franklin Falls is for you. Experience up close what happens when you mix water and gravity—feel the power. Hear the roar.

Wipe off your glasses—you're gonna get splashed. The only thing louder than the rush of water are the squeals of delighted children.

Getting There

Head east on Interstate 90 to Exit 47, about 16 miles east of North Bend, and head north. About 0.1 mile farther turn right at the T intersection. In about 0.25 mile, turn left onto Forest Road 58 (Denny Creek Road) and follow it for about 2.5 miles to the Denny Creek Campground. Just after the campground turn left into a large gravel parking lot. The trailhead is just before the bridge on the right. Elevation: 2,400 feet.

The Trail

Tell a kid to draw a waterfall and chances are he or she will draw something that looks like Franklin Falls. Here the South Fork of the Snoqualmie River just runs out of riverbed and plunges in a thrilling

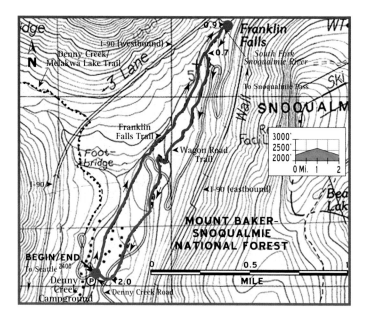

Franklin Falls is a walk-up wonder

PERMITS/CONTACT
Northwest Forest Pass required/Mount Baker–Snoqualmie National Forest,
North Bend Ranger District, (425) 888-1421

MAPS
USGS Snoqualmie Pass; Green Trails Snoqualmie Pass 207, Snoqualmie Pass
Gateway 207S

TRAIL NOTES
Leashed dogs okay; kid-friendly; great views; cool waterfall

70-foot horsetail of white water to a cool pool below. The canyon walls amplify the sound of both the falling water and the squealing kids who are awed by this giant faucet and the big trouble that somebody's going to be in for leaving it running like this. This is a popular place on weekends, but as with so many Puget Sound–region trails and natural attractions, during the week you pretty much have the run of the place.

From the trailhead follow the trail as it hugs the river and passes through dense, old-growth forest. At several points it rises high above the river atop the canyon wall. Caution: Several points along the rim of the gorge have steep drop-offs to the left with no guardrails or fences to keep visitors back. Keep young ones close; don't let them—or dogs for that matter—run ahead.

At a couple of points the trail approaches Denny Creek Road (and in fact pullouts on that road make for parking spots if you're more into the falls than you are into the hike there). At about **0.7** mile the trail reaches a signed intersection with the Wagon Road Trail; save this for the way back. Continue straight about a quarter-mile to reach the falls. The last few feet, with the rushing gush of Franklin Falls plunging over the cliff in view, require negotiating a somewhat narrow rock ledge that's likely to be slippery, if not from rain then from waterfall mist. Approach as close as you feel safe (and warm—the air seems fifteen degrees cooler in this shaded splash zone). Oddly, the westbound I-90 bridge rises high above the falls. But the water is so loud and awe-inspiring that you hardly even notice.

Return the same way, or for a loop experience, on the way back go left at the sign for Wagon Road Trail. In contrast to the popular Franklin Falls Trail, here you're likely to have the trail to yourself. This trail follows the old Snoqualmie Pass wagon road built in the 1860s. Take care as the trail crosses Denny Creek Road at several points. At **2.0** miles reach the trail end at Denny Creek Road, just across from the parking lot where you started. ∎

SNOQUALMIE PASS

57. Snow Lake

RATING	DISTANCE	HIKING TIME
★ ★ ★ ★ ☆	**6.0 miles round-trip**	**3 hours**

ELEVATION GAIN	HIGH POINT	DIFFICULTY
1,700 feet	**4,400 feet**	♦ ♦ ◇ ◇ ◇

BEST SEASON
Jan Feb Mar Apr May Jun **Jul Aug Sep Oct** Nov Dec

The Hike

This relatively easy hike, accessed via an easy-to-get-to trailhead with a massive parking lot, leads to a jewel of a lake in a gorgeous setting, and you know what that means—crowds. The US Forest Service calls Snow Lake "the most frequented trail in the Alpine Lakes Wilderness." But hey, if you're a people person—and a dog person—head here on a day that begins with "S," find a spot in the huge lot, and go for it. Otherwise, visit during the week. Just don't miss it—this trail's a treat.

Getting There

Head east on Interstate 90 to Exit 52 at Snoqualmie Pass, about 21 miles east of North Bend, and turn left under the freeway. Turn right on Alpental Road and continue for 1.5 miles to the large Alpental ski area parking lot. The trailhead is on the right. Elevation: 3,100 feet.

The Trail

After filling out the Alpine Lakes Wilderness Pass, find the trailhead across the road from the parking lot and begin by climbing an impressive set of wood stairs built over the years by Washington Trails Association. (Thanks, guys 'n' gals.) Your heart rate now elevated, traverse a mostly level stretch of forest, rock garden, and open meadow offering views first of Alpental's ski area, then Denny Mountain, Chair Peak, the Tooth, and a crown of rocky crags that surround you.

Continuing on, the trail climbs gradually across open slopes, occasionally rocky but always with spectacular views, and at **1.5** miles reaches a signed intersection. Go straight for about a half-mile for

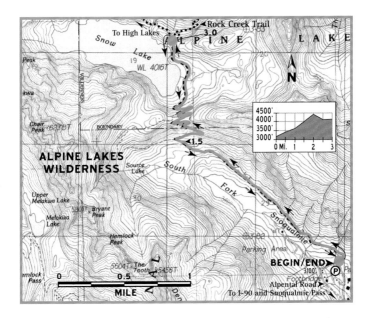

views of Source Lake, sitting like a drain in the bottom of a basin, and the source of . . . anybody? The South Fork Snoqualmie River, that's right.

To head to Snow Lake, go right at the intersection and begin climbing and switchbacking in earnest immediately. In about a mile,

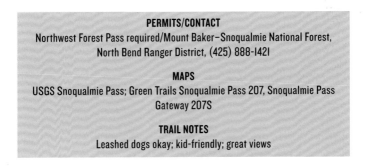

PERMITS/CONTACT
Northwest Forest Pass required/Mount Baker–Snoqualmie National Forest, North Bend Ranger District, (425) 888-1421

MAPS
USGS Snoqualmie Pass; Green Trails Snoqualmie Pass 207, Snoqualmie Pass Gateway 207S

TRAIL NOTES
Leashed dogs okay; kid-friendly; great views

Snow Lake is one of the most accessible in the Alpine Lakes Wilderness

just after entering the Alpine Lakes Wilderness, reach the top of the ridge and garner your first glimpse of Snow Lake. (Some folks find a spot on a nice rock and make this their turnaround point.) Follow the trail as it descends about 400 feet over the next half-mile to the lake. Once there, it's time to go into alpine lake mode—chill out, relax, lounge about, take 'er easy. Follow some of the numerous exploratory side trails, but also respect and *stay off!* those areas where trail restoration is taking place.

When you've had enough, return the same way.

Going Farther

On the north side of the lake a trail intersection offers a couple options. Go right for the Rock Creek Trail, which leads 4.3 miles and drops 2,500 feet on the way to the Middle Fork of the Snoqualmie River and the Middle Fork Trail. Go left for the High Lakes Trail, which leads first to Gem Lake, about 2 miles and 800 feet of elevation gain beyond Snow Lake. About 2 miles beyond that, after about a thousand feet of elevation *loss*, is Lower Wildcat Lake. Camping is available at the Denny Creek Campground, about 2 miles west of Exit 52 on Forest Road 58. ■

58. Lodge Lake

RATING	DISTANCE	HIKING TIME
★★★☆☆	4.0 miles round-trip	2 hours

ELEVATION GAIN	HIGH POINT	DIFFICULTY
900 feet	3,480 feet	♦♦◊◊◊

BEST SEASON											
Jan	Feb	Mar	Apr	May	Jun	Jul	Aug	Sep	Oct	Nov	Dec

The Hike

As this trail proves, first impressions can be deceiving. This pleasant hike starts near the hustle and bustle of Snoqualmie Pass, crosses ski slopes usually reserved for the one- and two-planked set, then leads into peaceful, contemplative forest, and finally arrives at a lake of the same demeanor. This is part of the Pacific Crest Trail.

Getting There

Head east on Interstate 90 to Exit 52 at Snoqualmie Pass, about 21 miles east of North Bend. Head south and take the first right, then first left into the large, gravel ski area parking lot. The trailhead is to the right (west), at the far end of the lot. Elevation: 3,000 feet.

The Trail

After a brief forested prologue, the trail swings to the left across a broad open ski slope. That might not sound like the most wilder-nessy of experiences, but "open slopes" implies views, which this one certainly has—north to Guye Peak, flanked by Snoqualmie and Red Mountains, east to Keechelus Lake and Eastern Washington beyond, and even down to the Indian paintbrush that appear to set this meadow aflame. To be honest, you'll also see the noisy freeway where semis and SUVs rumble from Western to Eastern Washington and vice versa. But that's easily remedied by putting shoe tread to trail and moving forward in a bipedal motion.

Follow the trail as it climbs the open slopes, passing the occasional service road but always easy to follow. At about **1.0** mile the

PERMITS/CONTACT
Northwest Forest Pass required/Mount Baker–Snoqualmie National Forest,
North Bend Ranger District, (425) 888-1421

MAPS
USGS Snoqualmie Pass; Green Trails Snoqualmie Pass 207, Snoqualmie Pass
Gateway 207S

TRAIL NOTES
Leashed dogs okay; kid-friendly; surprisingly quiet lakes

trail reaches a saddle and levels off just before reaching Beaver Lake. Although the sounds of the freeway have been left behind, you're still treated to mountain views. For small children or those new to hiking, this makes a nice lunch and turnaround point. Continuing past Beaver Lake, the trail enters forest for the first time since the prologue and almost immediately begins descending toward Lodge Lake. You lose about 350 feet (which you'll have to climb on the way out, of course) over the next mile, before reaching a signed intersection pointing the way to the lake, which is two skips and not even a hop away. (Because this is part of the Pacific Crest Trail, going straight could potentially land you in Mexico.)

Little-visited Lodge Lake seems far from the crowds at Snoqualmie Pass

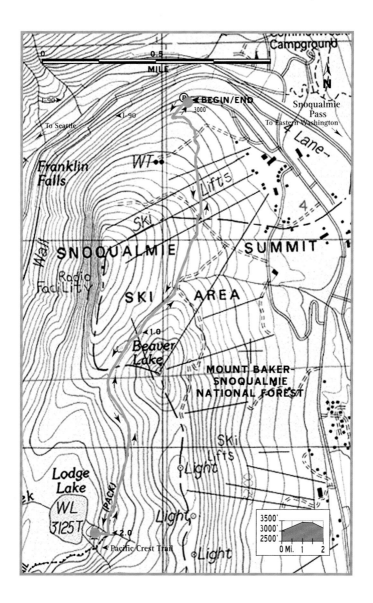

0

0.5

MILE

I-90►

◄I-90

To Seattle

Franklin
Falls

WT

Wall

Ski

Lifts

SNOQUALMIE

Radio
Facility

SKI

AREA

Cumuluwealt
Campground

N

Ⓟ ◄BEGIN/END
3000

Snoqualmie
Pass
To Eastern Washington

Lane-

SUMMIT

◄1.0

Beaver
Lake

MOUNT BAKER-
SNOQUALMIE
NATIONAL FOREST

Ski

Lifts

Light

Lodge
Lake

WL
3125 T

[PACK]

◄2.0

◄Pacific Crest Trail

Light

Light

3500'
3000'
2500'

0 Mi.   1   2

Explore and decompress at the lake. It's quiet here, and with most hikers heading off on trails on the north side of Snoqualmie Pass, you might just have some quality alone time, especially during the week. The lake was the site of a lodge built in 1914 by The Mountaineers to enjoy during ski outings. It burned down in 1944.

Return the same way, remembering that you have about 350 feet of elevation to make up.

Going Farther
Because this is part of the Pacific Crest Trail, the options for continuing past the lake are just about limitless. One popular turnaround spot is Olallie Meadow and Windy Pass, about 4 miles past Lodge Lake. Camping is available at the Denny Creek Campground, about 2 miles west of the trailhead off Forest Road 58. ■

59. Commonwealth Basin–Red Pass

RATING	DISTANCE	HIKING TIME
★★★★☆	10.0 miles round-trip	6 hours

ELEVATION GAIN	HIGH POINT	DIFFICULTY
2,600 feet	5,300 feet	♦♦♦◊◊

BEST SEASON
Jan Feb Mar Apr May Jun **Jul Aug Sep Oct** Nov Dec

The Hike
When the sun hits it, Red Mountain sticks out like a thumb that's been hammered. Thankfully, this pleasant forest and valley walk won't make you feel the same. Views of everything from Rainier to practically the North Cascades are terrific, and what's really nice is that while most people continue on the nearby Pacific Crest Trail, you might just have the basin and pass to yourself.

Red Mountain is a prominent peak on the PCT

Getting There

Head east on Interstate 90 to Exit 52 at Snoqualmie Pass, about 21 miles east of North Bend. Head north on Alpental Road. A few hundred yards ahead, turn right at the sign for the Pacific Crest Trail. Just ahead, take another right following the sign for Forest Road 9041. The parking lot is just ahead. Elevation: 3,000 feet.

PERMITS/CONTACT
Northwest Forest Pass required/Mount Baker–Snoqualmie National Forest, North Bend Ranger District, (425) 888-1421

MAPS
USGS Snoqualmie Pass; Green Trails Snoqualmie Pass 207, Snoqualmie Pass Gateway 207S

TRAIL NOTES
Leashed dogs okay; kid-friendly—to basin; great mountain views

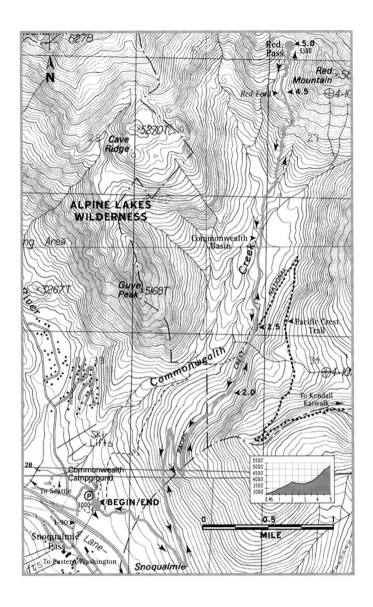

The Trail

From behind the trailhead kiosk follow the obvious trail for about 100 yards and turn right at an unmarked T intersection. The first 2.5 miles follows the Pacific Crest Trail—note the trailhead sign indicating that it's only 67 miles to Stevens Pass; if you're feeling burly, go for it—which means that the trail is easy to follow, well maintained, and perhaps takes a little more time than you're used to when gaining elevation. That's a good thing, right?

Enjoy the old-growth forest as the trail lazily switchbacks heading east, then due north, then due east, then north, and so on. Great views of Mount Rainier emerge on the south-facing swings. At about **2.0** miles descend for a quarter-mile as you traverse an open boulder field that just might be eyeing your knees and ankles for a snack. Step carefully, especially because you'll likely be looking up at the rusty pyramid of Red Mountain.

At **2.5** miles, shortly after reentering the forest, go left at a signed fork following the sign for Commonwealth Basin. Drop immediately for a bit into the forested basin accompanied by the gurgle-gurgle or swhoosh-whoosh (depending on the season) sound of Commonwealth Creek. Soon enough, the trail levels out as it bee-lines through the valley, eventually crossing the creek near a pleasant picnic and camping area. This makes a good turnaround spot for families with young children.

Once across the creek, the trail takes pains to remind you that you're no longer on the Pacific Crest Trail any more, boys and girls, and begins climbing in earnest, switchbacking steeply up the hillside. But it repays with huge views of Mount Rainier and closer peaks near Snoqualmie Pass and, depending on the season, wildflowers. At **4.5** miles the trail temporarily flattens out in a meadowy cirque, where just ahead Red Pond and its exploratory trails offer a respite from the climbing. Red Mountain rises high and to the right (east), with climbers likely making for its summit trying to do the same. The mountain's rock is not the most solid, however, so be aware that bits and pieces of Red Mountain often come tumbling down.

Red Pass is straight ahead, at **5.0** miles and 500 feet above. The homestretch consists of multiple switchbacks up talus slope. Reach the ridge crest and enjoy superb views north toward Mount Thompson (the prominent shark fin about two air miles away), down into the Middle Fork Snoqualmie River valley, and straight up at Red Mountain practically looming overhead. To the south views of the Snoqualmie Pass ski areas beckon and from this angle appear to be watched over by a beneficent Mount Rainier, which itself appears to float in the air like some unmoving, never-changing cloud. The actual pass is to the left a few yards, but views are grand from anywhere on the ridge.

Going Farther

This trail uses the same trailhead as the Pacific Crest Trail to Kendall Katwalk (Hike 60), and, in fact, the Commonwealth Basin–Red Pass Trail follows the Pacific Crest Trail for about the first 2.5 miles. Also, from the Red Pond meadow at about **4.5** miles, climbers often scramble to the top of Red Mountain itself. Although it's not considered a particularly technical climb, the mountain's loose rock and the prospect of getting clobbered by bits that fall down the mountain make it a potentially dangerous one. Camping is available at the Denny Creek Campground, about 3 miles west of the trailhead off Forest Road 58. ∎

60. Kendall Katwalk

RATING	DISTANCE	HIKING TIME
★ ★ ★ ★ ★	11.4 miles round-trip	6 hours

ELEVATION GAIN	HIGH POINT	DIFFICULTY
2,700 feet	5,400 feet	◆ ◆ ◆ ◇ ◇

BEST SEASON
Jan Feb Mar Apr May Jun **Jul Aug Sep Oct** Nov Dec

The Hike

Lots of people do a turn on the Kendall Katwalk, and for a number of good reasons. Rocky peaks, emerald valleys, and fields of wild-flowers, all watched over by a looming Mount Rainier—what could be better? Then there's the Katwalk, a narrow stretch of trail blasted into granite and featuring a drop-off that's an acrophobe's nightmare. Another draw is the gentle grade. The trail follows the Pacific Crest Trail, which does its darndest to keep the climbing to a minimum.

Getting There

Head east on Interstate 90 to Exit 52 at Snoqualmie Pass, about 21 miles east of North Bend. Head north on Alpental Road. A few hundred yards ahead, turn right at the sign for the Pacific Crest Trail. Just ahead, take another right following the sign for Forest Road 9041. The parking lot is just ahead. Elevation: 3,000 feet.

PERMITS/CONTACT
Northwest Forest Pass required/Mount Baker–Snoqualmie National Forest, North Bend Ranger District, (425) 888-1421

MAPS
USGS Snoqualmie Pass; Green Trails Snoqualmie Pass 207, Snoqualmie Pass Gateway 207S

TRAIL NOTES
Leashed dogs okay; great views

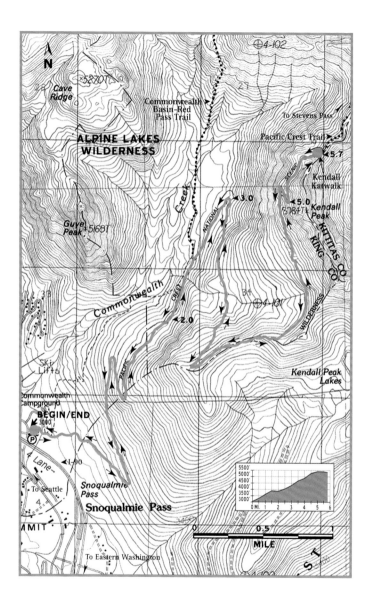

N

Cave
Ridge

*5870'

Commonwealth
Basin–Red
Pass Trail

⊕4-102

21

To Stevens Pass

Pacific Crest Trail

ALPINE LAKES
WILDERNESS

▲5.7

Kendall
Katwalk

▲5.0 Kendall
Peak

▲3.0

Guye
Peak *5168'

*5764'

KITTITAS CO.
KING CO.

Commonwealth

⊕4-101

B6

▲2.0

WILDERNESS

Kendall Peak
Lakes

Ski
Lifts

Commonwealth
Campground

BEGIN/END
3000'

Ⓟ

I-90

4 Lane

Snoqualmie
Pass

To Seattle

4

Snoqualmie Pass

MMIT

1

To Eastern Washington

5500'
5000'
4500'
4000'
3500'
3000'

0 MI. 1 2 3 4 5 6

0   0.5   1
MILE

ST

*4400

The Kendall Katwalk

The Trail

After filling out an Alpine Lakes Wilderness Pass at the trailhead, enter the forest. In about a hundred yards turn right at an unmarked T intersection. Continue as the trail narrows a bit and offers rocks and roots—as well as some not-too-staggering elevation gain—for your enjoyment.

Enjoy the old-growth forest as the trail lazily switchbacks heading east, then due north, then due east, then north, and so forth. Great views of Mount Rainier emerge on the south-facing swings. At about **2.0** miles descend for a quarter-mile as you traverse an open boulder field that just might be eyeing your knees and ankles for a snack. Step carefully, especially because you'll likely be looking up at the rusty pyramid of Red Mountain.

Shortly after a sign indicates that you've entered the Alpine Lakes Wilderness Area, bear right at a fork and a sign for Pacific Crest Trail. The Commonwealth Basin–Red Pass Trail (Hike 59) is the one to the left. Begin climbing steeply and as you pass through a semi-open area, marvel at Red Mountain straight ahead looking so red it boggles the head. The trail makes an abrupt 180-degree turn south at **3.0** miles but continues climbing steadily. When trees and avalanche chutes allow, peek at peaks all around. Truly inspiring. Return to forest for about a mile-and-a-half and when next you emerge, the views are even more inspiring. Peaks and meadows and wildflowers seem to stretch to infinity. Below, check out the freeway and Snoqualmie's ski areas. Ahead, when the trail again swings back toward the south, Rainier's frosty visage seems to be at eye level.

Soon the trail becomes a narrow ledge, climbing steeply along an exposed rock garden. Concentration is key. At **5.0** miles the route makes an abrupt turn to the east (right) and levels off for a bit. Just ahead on the right is a nice view and picnic spot, but with the Katwalk not far ahead, hit it on the way back. At **5.7** miles reach the Katwalk, a narrow ledge blasted through granite that's almost guaranteed to annoy your inner acrophobe.

Return the same way.

Going Farther

This trail uses the same trailhead as the Commonwealth Basin–Red Pass Trail (Hike 59) and the Pacific Crest Trail, which continues onto across the US-Canada border near Manning Park. Another good day-hike turnaround point is the saddle between Ridge and Gravel Lakes, about 2 miles past and 400 feet below Kendall Katwalk. Camping is available at the Denny Creek Campground, about 3 miles west of the trailhead off Forest Road 58. ■

61. Snoqualmie Tunnel

RATING	DISTANCE	HIKING TIME
★★★☆☆	5.2 miles round-trip	2 hours
ELEVATION GAIN	**HIGH POINT**	**DIFFICULTY**
100 feet	2,600 feet	◆◇◇◇◇
BEST SEASON		
Jan Feb Mar Apr May **Jun Jul Aug Sep Oct** Nov Dec		

The Hike

This trail offers hands-down the best opportunity for tunnel hiking of any trail in this book, bar none. And it's probably best for giving one the willies, too. If you're not afraid of a little darkness, strap on a headlamp or carry a flashlight and venture inside. You'll come out at the other side of the state.

Getting There

Head east on Interstate 90 to Exit 54, about 2 miles east of Snoqualmie Pass. From the exit take a right and then a quick left onto Spur 906. (Follow signs for Snoqualmie Tunnel.) Go right in 0.5 mile; the Hyak trailhead parking lot is just ahead. Elevation: 2,600 feet.

PERMITS/CONTACT
Discover Pass required/Lake Easton State Park (they take calls for Iron Horse State Park including Snoqualmie Tunnel), (509) 656-2230

MAPS
USGS Snoqualmie Pass; Green Trails Snoqualmie Pass 207, Snoqualmie Pass Gateway 207S

TRAIL NOTES
Leashed dogs okay; great views; kid-friendly—kinda; darkness like you wouldn't believe

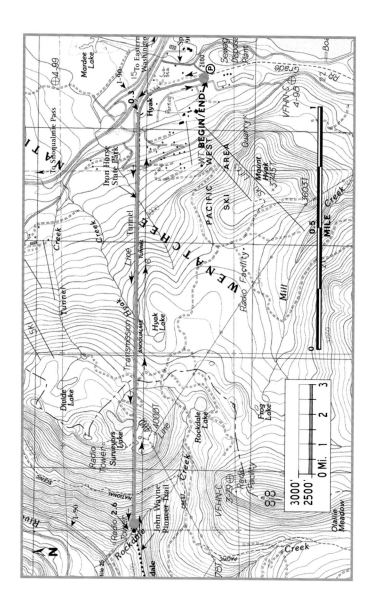

Damp, dark, and cold—what's not to love about a visit to the Snoqualmie Tunnel

The Trail

From the trailhead follow the way-wide rail trail (the former Chicago–Milwaukee–St. Paul Pacific Railroad line) to the right (west) for about 0.3 mile to the tunnel's east entrance. Along the way check out interpretive signs that detail the railway's heyday in the 1930s and 1940s as the ski train from Seattle and Tacoma. Built in 1912 and opened to the public for walking and biking in 1994, it's the longest tunnel for nonmotorized use in the United States. (Oh really. We thought it might've been uh . . . , well there's . . . , and uh, . . . How many tunnel trails are there that are open to the public?)

Also, as the interpretive signs tell you, the rail trail on which you're walking is now called the John Wayne Pioneer Trail (Hike 41), named for the late actor because, as the sign says, he "symbolizes for many the positive spirit of the West."

Back to the tunnel. Upon entering, note the darkness, the blackness, the sheer nothingness. But also note the sound of dripping water, the wind whipping your face, and that tiny pinprick of light way, way down there. That would be the west entrance of the tunnel, 2.3 miles away on the other side of Snoqualmie Pass. Go for it. But before you do, take heed of some advice. Take a flashlight and extra batteries and a jacket. Even on the hottest days, it can be quite chilly inside, and there's always a breeze from the west. Once you've made it to the west entrance, turn around and return the same way.

Going Farther

To make this a point-to-point hike, park one car at the Hyak parking lot and another at the Asahel Curtis–Annette Lake trailhead (Hikes 53 and 54). After hiking west through the tunnel, continue for another 1.5 miles to the intersection of the rail trail and Annette Lake. Go right and reach the Annette Lake trailhead parking lot in about 0.7 mile. ■

62. Mount Catherine

RATING	DISTANCE	HIKING TIME
★★★☆☆	2.4 miles round-trip	2 hours

ELEVATION GAIN	HIGH POINT	DIFFICULTY
1,300 feet	5,052 feet	◆◆◇◇◇

BEST SEASON
Jan Feb Mar Apr May **Jun Jul Aug Sep Oct** Nov Dec

The Hike
Steep but short and with 360-degree views that'll make vista hogs happy (that is, if they can ignore the clear-cuts), Mount Catherine is an oft-overlooked treat. Located near the Pacific Crest Trail, from the summit you feel like you're straddling the state. Looking north toward Snoqualmie Pass, Keechelus Lake and dryish Eastern Washington are on your right, and rain- and snow-soaked Western Washington is on your left. On clear days look for Mount Rainier to the south.

Getting There
Head east on Interstate 90 to Exit 54, about 2 miles east of Snoqualmie Pass. From the exit, go right and then enter the Summit East Ski Area. Follow the road for a total of 5.1 miles. (At first it curves to the left, then passes through some vacation properties, and at 0.7 mile turns to gravel and becomes Forest Road 9070.) The easy-to-miss,

PERMITS/CONTACT
Northwest Forest Pass required/Okanogan-Wenatchee National Forest, Cle Elum Ranger District, (509) 852-1100

MAPS
USGS Lost Lake; Green Trails Snoqualmie Pass 206, Snoqualmie Pass Gateway 207S

TRAIL NOTES
Leashed dogs okay; kid-friendly; great views

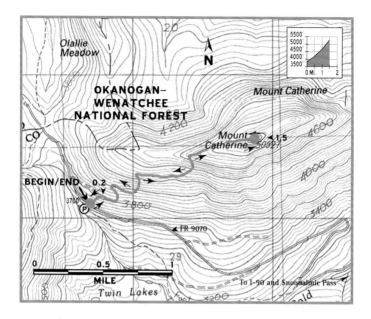

small-signed trailhead at 5.1 miles is on the right; a small roadside parking lot is on the left. Elevation: 3,700 feet.

The Trail

Begin by climbing steeply through a clear-cut up a former logging road—with tiny trees growing in the middle of it—which, soon enough, becomes a true trail. At about **0.2** mile go straight at an intersection (a sign just ahead confirms you're on the right path) and soon enter forest.

At **1.0** mile the grade lessens a tad as the trail reaches a ridge and offers the first views north, albeit somewhat obstructed, toward Snoqualmie Pass. Over the next mile, the trail follows the ridge climbing not-too-badly, and approaches an open, former cabin spot, accessorized by bits of twisted metal. That's the theme for the final steep stretch to the top.

Views of Keechelus Lake and Eastern Washington from Mount Catherine

Mount Catherine is the site of a former airway beacon, and pieces of an old cable overlay the rocky scramble to the top. It's a good thing, too. The final push requires hands as well as feet, so anything that offers a better handhold is welcome. The top is a mini summit, just short of a mile high, and the 360-degree views are grand and unobstructed. Snap away with the camera; you can Photoshop away those clear-cuts later. ■

63. Gold Creek Pond

RATING	DISTANCE	HIKING TIME
★★☆☆☆	1.0-mile lollipop loop	30 minutes
ELEVATION GAIN	**HIGH POINT**	**DIFFICULTY**
40 feet	2,550 feet	◆◇◇◇◇
BEST SEASON		
Jan Feb Mar Apr May Jun Jul Aug Sep Oct Nov Dec		

The Hike

I'm reminded of the Talking Heads song with the line "Once there were parking lots, now it's a peaceful oasis." Gold Creek Pond was a onetime gravel pit; now it's a small mountain lake featuring a barrier-free interpretive trail that offers everyone the alpine experience. Views extend deep into Gold Creek valley and the Alpine Lakes Wilderness, making it a great place for a picnic.

Getting There

Go east on Interstate 90 to Exit 54, about 2 miles east of Snoqualmie Pass, and go left at the end of the exit ramp and continue for 0.2 mile. Turn right onto Forest Road 4832 (follow the sign for Gold Creek), which parallels the freeway, and in 0.9 mile turn left onto gravel Gold

PERMITS/CONTACT
Northwest Forest Pass required/Mount Baker–Snoqualmie National Forest, North Bend Ranger District, (425) 888-1421

MAPS
USGS Snoqualmie Pass; Green Trails Snoqualmie Pass 207, Snoqualmie Pass Gateway 207S

TRAIL NOTES
Leashed dogs okay; kid-friendly; great views; barrier-free; picnic tables and barbecues

This was a gravel pit; now it's a pond on Gold Creek

Creek Road (FR 142) at the sign for Gold Creek Pond. In 0.5 mile turn left on a paved road (that appears to be a mirage) that leads a few hundred yards to the large trailhead parking lot. Elevation: 2,550 feet.

The Trail

From the large parking lot, follow the paved path as it follows the edge of the forest paralleling Gold Creek. This is the stick for this lollipop loop; reach the sucker in about 100 yards, near a semi-vast lakeside picnic area. Pick a direction and follow it; either way leads back to where you are now.

Following the loop (either way), huge views open up immediately. Straight ahead, the Gold Creek valley cuts a wide swath between Rampart Ridge on the right and Kendall Peak and her neighbors on the left. Behind you is Mount Catherine and the lifts of the Summit East Ski Area. The lake itself is likely to be all a-gaggle with geese, who nest and frolic like the wild geese they are on an island in the middle of the pond. (On an early May morning, I had no choice but to listen to a pair of amorous geese attempting to work things out

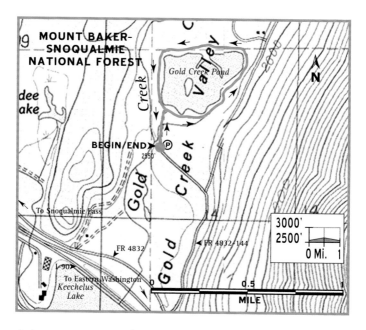

Gold Creek Pond

MOUNT BAKER-
SNOQUALMIE
NATIONAL FOREST

dee
ake

Creek

Gold Creek Valley

N

BEGIN/END
2550'

Gold

Creek

To Snoqualmie Pass

FR 4832

FR 4832-144

Gold

To Eastern Washington
Keechelus
Lake

3000'
2500'

0 Mi.   1

0   0.5   1

MILE

during my entire visit.) About halfway around the loop, an exploratory trail leads a short way along a mini spit into the middle of the lake. In various spots twisted bits of metal, evidence of the pond's former life, can be seen at the bottom of the pond. Follow the loop around, enjoy a peaceful picnic, and take in some fine mountain scenery. ■

64. Rachel Lake

RATING	DISTANCE	HIKING TIME
★★★★☆	7.6 miles round-trip	5 hours
ELEVATION GAIN	**HIGH POINT**	**DIFFICULTY**
1,900 feet	4,700 feet	◆◆◆◆◇
BEST SEASON		
Jan Feb Mar Apr May Jun Jul Aug Sep Oct Nov Dec		

The Hike

A popular family destination (meaning if privacy is your main concern, go somewhere else), this trail has much to recommend it beyond just a stunning, rock-rimmed alpine lake. Along the way waterfalls and giant rocks on which to bask, if not immerse yourself in said falls, invite attention.

Getting There

Go east on Interstate 90 to Exit 62, about 10 miles east of Snoqualmie Pass and turn left, following the sign for Kachess Campground. Follow Kachess Lake Road for 5.2 miles to Forest Road 4930, just outside Kachess Campground, and turn left. Follow the road for 4 miles to the road-end trailhead parking lot. Elevation: 2,800 feet.

The Trail

Find the trailhead on the opposite (north) side of the road from the parking lot. Enter the forest and start by climbing immediately up rocky, root-riddled, and what's likely to be dusty trail. Shortly after crossing a creek pouring down from Hi Box Lake, the trail meets up with Box Canyon Creek, which will accompany the trail—facilitate it if you will—for much of the rest of the way. As creekside trails often do, the grade lessens a bit.

Box Canyon drains both Box and Rampart Ridges, and as a result the sound of rushing water is everywhere. So are some marshy damp spots—passable via some rocks and log bridges—and, at certain times of the year, those of the pesky black fly and skeeter persuasion.

Rachel Lake is the perfect place to cool off on summer afternoons

At **1.0** mile the trail swings toward the creek and some massive, moss-toupeed boulders that are the size of humpback whale backs. Box Creek spills down huge, flat, pockmarked whale backs, which, when the water level cooperates, make for a great picnic and water-play spot.

Views to Rampart Ridge emerge as the trail gently follows the creek and crosses a couple of areas likely to be overgrown. At **2.3** miles, after crossing a few creeks in quick succession, the trail strikes the phrase "climbs gradually" from its vocabulary and replaces it with "powers its way in a near-vertical, switchbacking fashion up the side of the

PERMITS/CONTACT
Northwest Forest Pass required/Wenatchee National Forest,
Cle Elum Ranger District, (509) 852-1100

MAPS
USGS Chikamin Peak; Green Trails Snoqualmie Pass 207

TRAIL NOTES
Leashed dogs okay; kid-friendly; great views; waterfalls; spectacular lake

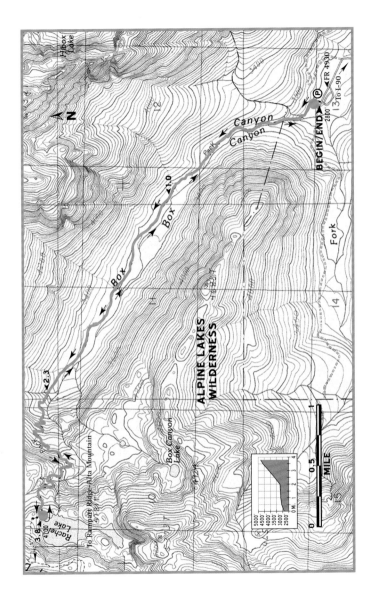

mountain." The trail closely parallels the creek, which, given the grade, is mostly a waterfall. Several spots on the way up allow for taking a few steps toward it and dunking one's head into the falling water.

At spots, open views to nearby Hi Box Mountain and faraway Mount Rainier offer distraction and seem to lessen the grade a bit. Along the way the trail crosses the creek and again, depending on the water level, this is a great place to lollygag either in, or beside, a tumbling waterfall. At **3.8** miles reach the lake, an alpine gem by the rocky cliffs of Rampart Ridge. Take a dip if the weather warrants, or circulate via exploratory trails heading off in both directions.

Going Farther
The Rampart Ridge–Alta Mountain Trail (Hike 65) uses the same trailhead and follows the Rachel Lake Trail as far as Rachel Lake. Camping is available at Kachess Lake Campground, about 4 miles south of the trailhead on the way in. ∎

65. Rampart Ridge–Alta Mountain

RATING	DISTANCE	HIKING TIME
★★★★★	12.0 miles round-trip	7 hours
ELEVATION GAIN	**HIGH POINT**	**DIFFICULTY**
3,600 feet	6,151 feet	◆◆◆◆◇
	BEST SEASON	
Jan Feb Mar Apr May Jun	Jul Aug Sep Oct	Nov Dec

The Hike
There might not be gold in them thar hills above Rachel Lake, but there certainly are views—and more lakes, too. Wander the ridge one way for the eponymous Rampart Lakes, go the other for Lila Lakes, and if you've got a scrambling jones, head up the ridge to Alta Mountain. If you do, big-time views of Mount Rainier and even Mount Adams come along for the ride.

Getting There

Go east on Interstate 90 to Exit 62, about 10 miles east of Snoqualmie Pass, and turn left, following the sign for Kachess Campground. Follow Kachess Lake Road for 5.2 miles to Forest Road 4930, just outside Kachess Campground, and turn left. Follow the road for 4 miles to the road-end trailhead parking lot. Elevation: 2,800 feet.

The Trail

Find the trailhead on the opposite (north) side of the road from the parking lot and begin climbing immediately up rocky, root-riddled, and what's likely to be dusty trail. Follow the trail—which follows Box Canyon Creek for much of the way—for 3.8 miles to Rachel Lake (Hike 64).

At the lake bear to the right, and follow as the trail turns a bit rugged on ya' over the next half-mile gaining elevation—and likely losing much of the crowds—like nobody's business. You're climbing Rampart Ridge here, my friend, climbing 600 feet or so in less than a half-mile. Turn around and take a breath from time to time, strengthening yourself with the superb views that improve exponentially with each step. Rachel Lake is a shimmering jewel tucked on a mountainside, and would tumble down the hillside were it not for the benevolence of lakeside trees and the boulders. Alta Mountain and Hi Box Peak are like Rachel's big brothers, keeping an eye on her at all times. To the south Mount Rainier pokes its head over Rampart Ridge, always in the mood to upstage smaller mountains. It's like a projected image in Nature's PowerPoint presentation.

PERMITS/CONTACT
Northwest Forest Pass required/Wenatchee National Forest, Cle Elum Ranger District, (509) 852-1100

MAPS
USGS Chikamin Peak; Green Trails Snoqualmie Pass 207

TRAIL NOTES
Leashed dogs okay; great views; some scrambling

Hi Box Ridge rises high above Lila Lake

At **4.3** miles reach the ridge. You're given a choice: go left for about a mile that gently roller-coasters up and down through peaceful meadowland (that is, heather 'n' blueberries) to Rampart Lakes and just beyond to the Rampart Ridge crest. Views of lake upon lake, tarn upon tarn, and peak upon peak are spectacular. Or you can go right, which is where I like to go, to the top of Alta Mountain.

Anytime there's an opportunity to make it to the top of something with the word "peak" or "mountain" in it and getting to the top requires about as much technical skill as does checking my mailbox, I go for it. For Alta follow the ridgetop trail, across the top of giant rock outcrops—which afford some of the best Rachel Lake views of the day and in fact make a great turnaround spot—for about a third of a mile to a fork in a heathery area. (Note: This fork is easy to miss.) Go right for Lila Lakes, tucked in a wonderland basin at the foot of Hi Box Mountain. It's hard not to want to wander down there, what with the huge lakeside boulders and exploratory trails that wander in and out of the trees.

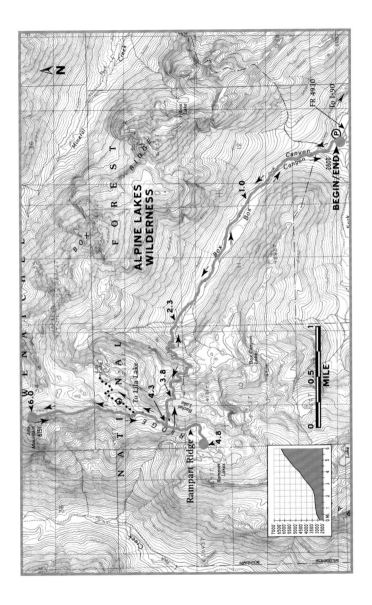

For Alta Mountain go left and take note how the trail climbs extremely steeply. (Okay, maybe it's a little harder than checking my mailbox, but it's just for a short stretch.) Soon enough the trail reaches the ridgetop, opening up a huge can of peak views to the north and west. Red Mountain is just so, so . . . red! You're in 360-view land here, and far, far to the south, Mount Adams shyly peers over the hills, as if not wanting Rainier to notice. In the nearer distance that's I-90's Hyak exit at the far end of the Gold Creek valley.

Wander along the ridge for as far as you're comfortable—once you're on the crest, views don't significantly improve the farther you go—and at about **6.0** miles reach Alta's rocky, craggy crown.

Going Farther

The Rachel Lake Trail (Hike 64) uses the same trailhead. Camping is available at Kachess Lake Campground, about 4 miles south of the trailhead on the way in. ■

CLE ELUM/TEANAWAY

66. Paddy-Go-Easy Pass

RATING	DISTANCE	HIKING TIME
★★★★☆	6.0 miles round-trip	4 hours

ELEVATION GAIN	HIGH POINT	DIFFICULTY
2,700 feet	6,085 feet	◆◆◆◆

BEST SEASON
Jan Feb Mar Apr May Jun **Jul Aug Sep Oct** Nov Dec

The Hike

Let it be said: the trail to Paddy-Go-Easy Pass is certainly not easy. (Please don't hit me.) It's steep, relentlessly so, but not superlong, and offers spectacular views along down to the marshy Cle Elum River valley, which looks like something out of the Alps. There is also Mount Daniel and Cathedral Rock, too, which from this side of the valley looks almost puny compared with Danny Boy. Views to the east are of row upon row of peak after peak.

Getting There

Go east on Interstate 90 to Exit 80, about 28 miles east of Snoqualmie Pass, and turn left (north) over the freeway. Follow it for 2.8 miles to Highway 903 (Salmon la Sac Road) and turn left, following the sign for Salmon la Sac. Continue for 16.6 miles to Salmon la Sac Campground and turn right onto Forest Road 4330. The signed Paddy-Go-Easy Pass trailhead parking lot is 11.3 miles ahead on the right. Elevation: 3,400 feet.

PERMITS/CONTACT
Northwest Forest Pass required/Wenatchee National Forest, Cle Elum Ranger District, (509) 852-1100

MAPS
USGS The Cradle; Green Trails Stevens Pass 176

TRAIL NOTES
Leashed dogs okay; great views; horses okay

Views from Paddy-Go-Easy Pass require a not-so-easy climb

The Trail

Begin by climbing steeply right out of the parking lot. Continue through the midparts by doing much of the same. Finally, polish this trail off at ridgetop by doing the same thing that got you there. Get the picture? Of course, there are advantages to a trail that behaves like Paddy-Go-Easy, and by that I mean climbing at about 900 feet per mile. It's not for everybody, so you're not so likely to be

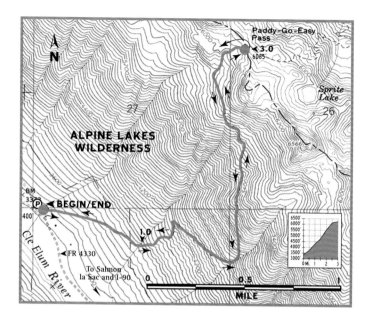

sniffed intimately or growled at by fourteen different Fidos whose owners wonder why you're getting irritated. You're likely to get lonesome even. And because the trail climbs so fast, you're going to have open, high-mountain vistas almost before you know it. (Okay, maybe not that fast, but close.)

Lower down the trail can be brushy and overgrown and at about **1.0** mile it crosses a creek, which can be a bit tricky. Trekking poles come in handy here. Just ahead, views begin opening up as the trail approaches subalpine meadow. Fish Lake and the Cle Elum River valley are stunning. In much of the Central Cascades you're used to seeing raging rivers busting through boulders and snags. Here's one that snakes through a marshland, like a slice of the Everglades in the Northwest.

As the trail swings north, Cathedral Rock and the icy glaciers and rocky ridges of Mount Daniel dominate. Continue climbing steadily in and out of pine forest, with wildflowers painting the hillsides, at times maneuvering up trail that has all the charm of a dry creekbed. If yours is to wonder why, just look up and the views will answer why you're hiking this steep and potentially hot (bring lots of water) trail.

Nearing the top, the trail winds through a semi-open boulder field, where trees fight for space among huge reddish boulders. At **3.0** miles reach the pass and its awesome front-row views of the 7,467-foot Cradle Massif. That's the French Creek valley leading north to the left, dampening the toes of numerous peaks. To the east Cashmere Mountain, of Icicle Gorge fame, can be spotted. If you want to throw a lake into the mix, head southeast for about a quarter-mile to Sprite Lake, a pleasant and easy side trip.

Going Farther

Camping is available at Fish Lake Campground, about 1 mile before the trailhead on Forest Road 4330, and at several campgrounds on Salmon la Sac Road, including Salmon la Sac Campground. ■

67. Cathedral Rock

RATING	DISTANCE	HIKING TIME
★★★★	**9.0 miles round-trip**	**5 hours**
ELEVATION GAIN	**HIGH POINT**	**DIFFICULTY**
2,250 feet	**5,600 feet**	◆◆◆◆
	BEST SEASON	
	Jan Feb Mar Apr May Jun **Jul Aug Sep Oct** Nov Dec	

The Hike

This trail leads to magical tarn- and heather-strewn parkland, where pond upon pond reflects the massive visage of Cathedral Rock. Views across the Cle Elum River valley to the Wenatchee Mountains are tops, and along the way Squaw Lake invites you to stop and take a moment to decompress.

Getting There

Go east on Interstate 90 to Exit 80, about 28 miles east of Snoqualmie Pass, and turn left (north) over the freeway. Follow for 2.8 miles to Highway 903 (Salmon la Sac Road) and turn left, following the sign for Salmon la Sac. Continue for 16.6 miles to Salmon la Sac Campground and turn right onto Forest Road 4330. The road-end Tucquala Meadows trailhead parking lot is 12.3 miles ahead. Elevation: 3,400 feet.

The Trail

The parking lot is also the trailhead for Deception Pass Trail (not to be confused with the narrow channel separating Fidalgo and Whidbey Islands), so first up make sure you find the right trail. It's the one heading west in the direction of the Cle Elum River. Both trails are signed, so there shouldn't be any confusion. Cross the Cle Elum via a spiffy wood bridge and enter cool forest. At first the trail doesn't climb much, and although you're well east of Snoqualmie Pass, the dense western red cedar–Douglas fir forest feels like you're still on the west (wet) side. That's because you pretty much still are. On a map you're fewer than 15 miles due south of Stevens Pass. Nothing like a little map-related minutia to give you something to think about while you're hiking the forest.

After the first few flat couple hundred yards or so, the trail begins climbing the ridge in long, somewhat steep, sweeping switchbacks. Partial views through the trees offer look-sees east to the chalky-looking Wenatchee Mountains, which look about as east side

PERMITS/CONTACT
Northwest Forest Pass required/Wenatchee National Forest, Cle Elum Ranger District, (509) 852-1100

MAPS
USGS The Cradle, Mount Daniel; Green Trails Stevens Pass 176

TRAIL NOTES
Leashed dogs okay; great views of Cathedral Rock; peaceful tarns

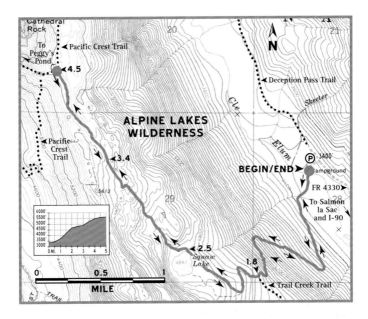

(dry) as the forest you're in does west (wet). (Oddly, switch number three seems to be intended to give you a break, as parts of it are almost flat.)

At **1.8** miles reach an intersection with the Trail Creek Trail (the sign says "Michael Lake Trail") and turn right. The trail levels off for a stretch, climbs steeply, then again attains a somewhat level ridge as it heads north. Mini spurs to the right offer open views down to the Cle Elum River valley, but keep going: Squaw Lake is just ahead at **2.5** miles. This peaceful, cliff-lined lake appears with no warning, like a mirage, and makes a great picnic and turnaround spot for those with children or without a lot of time.

To continue on, follow the shoreline to the right, rockhopping for a bit and crossing some perpetually muddy and marshy spots, and resume climbing steeply above the lake. At about **3.4** miles reach the start of a pleasant meadow and rock garden area that'll have you slowing down to enjoy a magical mountain setting. Heather and

Cathedral Rock against the backdrop of Mount Daniel

blueberry bushes and big rock slabs invite stopping and soaking it all in. Continue on for more of the same, bolstered by a line of tiny tarns you come to on the right, views east to craggy ridges, and, at the head of it all, looming 6,724-foot Cathedral Rock. Follow the ridge, amazed as you'll no doubt be, at peaks that seem to unfold in front of you—glacier-clad Mount Daniel inspiring a gape or two and Mount Stuart not far behind.

This is land for lollygagging, and you're welcome to do so on the many exploratory trails that head this way and that. But be sure to stay on trails and keep off those where signs say restoration work is being done. At **4.5** miles reach a signed intersection with the Pacific Crest Trail, which makes a good turnaround point.

Going Farther

A 15-mile loop can be made by going right at the intersection with the Pacific Crest Trail and following it for 5.2 miles to Deception Pass. From there head south for 5 miles to the Tucquala Meadows trailhead, where you parked. Another popular option is to hike west for about 1 mile from the Pacific Crest Trail intersection to Peggy's Pond. Although short, this path is primitive, steep, and can be a bit scary.

A few primitive campsites are available at the trailhead. Otherwise, camping is available at Fish Lake Campground, about 2 miles before the trailhead, and at several campgrounds on Salmon la Sac Road, including Salmon la Sac Campground. ■

68. Longs Pass

RATING	DISTANCE	HIKING TIME
★ ★ ★ ★ ★	6.0 miles round-trip	4 hours

ELEVATION GAIN	HIGH POINT	DIFFICULTY
1,900 feet	6,200 feet	♦ ♦ ♦ ◇ ◇

BEST SEASON
Jan Feb Mar Apr May Jun **Jul Aug Sep Oct** Nov Dec

The Hike

If it's Mount Stuart views you want, take the short but steep route to Longs Pass. From the pass, the state's second highest nonvolcanic peak is just three raven-flight miles across Ingalls Creek and appears close enough to hit with a rock. Turn around and that blindingly white mass the other way is Mount Rainier.

Getting There

Go east on Interstate 90 to Exit 85, about 33 miles east of Snoqualmie Pass. Head left (north) toward Cle Elum and in 0.2 mile turn right onto Highway 970. Follow that east for 6.6 miles to Teanaway Road and turn left. Follow that for 22.7 miles to the road-end trailhead (following signs for Esmeralda Basin or Trail 1394). The first 13 miles of road are paved; the last 9.7 (when it becomes Forest Road 9737) are gravel. The road washed out in 2016 and underwent extensive repairs. Before heading out, call the Cle Elum Ranger District for the current status. Elevation: 4,200.

The Trail

The trailhead is surrounded by high peaks and ridges, which on summer mornings can play tricks on you, blocking the sun and making you think the trail will be as chilly as you are now when you step out of your car. Don't believe it. This is Eastern Washington, where triple-digit temps are not uncommon. Beneath the regal visage of the Esmeralda Peaks, enter the forest and begin climbing via the creek-paralleling Esmeralda Basin Trail. Go slow, take 'er easy, let them calves 'n' quads wake up. Take note of the reddish rock that's tumbled from slopes above and appears to have been poured like sand into the forest and craggy outcrops below.

At **0.4** mile go right at the signed intersection with the Ingalls Way Trail (Hike 69) and begin switchbacking steeply up semi-open pine forest. ("I love the smell of Eastern Washington pine forest in the morning. It smells like . . . victory"—I've more than once found myself on trails like this amending the words to *Apocalypse Now*.) The higher you climb, the lower the Esmeralda Peaks become, those that seemed to tower over you so dauntingly at the trailhead, and check out views south toward Teanaway Ridge and the Teanaway

PERMITS/CONTACT
Northwest Forest Pass required/Wenatchee National Forest,
Cle Elum Ranger District, (509) 852-1100

MAPS
USGS Mount Stuart; Green Trails Mount Stuart 209

TRAIL NOTES
No dogs allowed; kid-friendly; the best Mount Stuart views with the least amount of work

Straight-on views of Mount Stuart from Longs Pass

River valley. It's a steep climb, as one would expect from a trail leading to front-row views of the Stuart Range.

At **2.4** miles go right at the signed intersection with the Longs Pass Trail. The trail is narrower, a little steeper even, at times side-hilling across bare, sandy slopes, but soon enough the trail surprises with views of hoary-topped Mount Rainier, still mega-prominent this far east. It follows an old mining road from the 1930s and for short stretches follows a latter-day jeep route seemingly straight up the side of the mountain.

Continue climbing, passing through a garden of reddish boulders, with Mount Adams views emerging to the south as a counterpoint to much larger Mount Rainier. After a couple of last steep stretches, you reach the pass at **3.0** miles and super views of Mount Stuart. In much the way that Mount Shuksan is arrayed to make

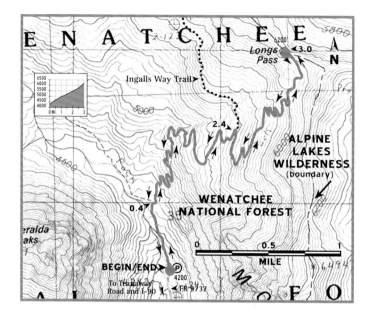

Heather Meadows just about the perfect place to view it, Longs Pass's straight-on prospect makes it just about the perfect place to view Mount Stuart. An argument can be made for Ingalls Lake; hike that trail and decide for yourself.

It's like you're backstage at the Stuart Range—Dragontail Peak and Little Annapurna are right there in front of you, but they look nothing like they do from the Colchuck Lake–Enchantments side of the world. Far down below your feet, the Ingalls Creek valley leads many miles east into Peshastin Creek and the Wenatchee River.

Going Farther

The Ingalls Way Trail uses the same trailhead and follows the same trail as the Longs Pass Trail for 2.6 miles. Also, the Esmeralda Basin Trail starts from the same trailhead. Camping is available at several campgrounds along Teanaway Road, the closest being Beverly Campground, about 4 miles before the trailhead on Forest Road 9737. ∎

69. Ingalls Way Trail

RATING	DISTANCE	HIKING TIME
★★★★★	10.8 miles round-trip	7 hours

ELEVATION GAIN	HIGH POINT	DIFFICULTY
2,600 feet	6,500 feet	◆◆◆◆◇

BEST SEASON
Jan Feb Mar Apr May Jun **Jul Aug Sep Oct** Nov Dec

The Hike

Top five in my book. (Maybe top three.) And judging from the weekend crowds, it's top five in a lot of people's books. But who can blame them? Mount Stuart is large and in charge, its reflection mirrored in a jewel of an azure, rock-lined lake that simply takes your breath away.

Getting There

Go east on Interstate 90 to Exit 85, about 33 miles east of Snoqualmie Pass. Head left (north) toward Cle Elum and in 0.2 mile turn right onto Highway 970. Follow it east for 6.6 miles to Teanaway Road and turn left. Follow it for 22.7 miles to the road-end trailhead following signs for Esmeralda Basin or Trail 1394. The first 13 miles of road are paved; the last 9.7 miles (when it becomes Forest Road 9737) are gravel. The road washed out in 2016 and underwent extensive repairs. Before heading out, call the Cle Elum Ranger District for the current status. Elevation: 4,200.

PERMITS/CONTACT
Northwest Forest Pass required/Wenatchee National Forest,
Cle Elum Ranger District, (509) 852-1100

MAPS
USGS Mount Stuart; Green Trails Mount Stuart 209

TRAIL NOTES
No dogs allowed; great lake and Stuart Range views

An Ingalls Lake lunch with Mount Stuart overhead

The Trail

The first 2.4 miles of this trail follow the same trails as does Longs Pass (Hike 68). Otherwise, start by following the Esmeralda Basin Trail for 0.4 mile to the signed intersection with the Ingalls Way Trail. Turn right and begin switchbacking steeply up semi-open pine forest. At **2.4** miles go straight at a signed intersection following the sign for the Ingalls Way Trail.

The trail contours along the open slope, with terrific views along the way, crossing boulder fields while steadily gaining elevation. You'll pass occasional stands of stubborn trees and bright red Indian paintbrush, but mostly it's open and rocky (red rocks at that) and all that suggests—heat, little water, and unobstructed views to far-off places like Mounts Rainier and Adams. The boulders get bigger the higher you go, and at times the way resembles less a trail than a primitive creekbed. At **3.9** miles upon entering the Alpine Lakes Wilderness, reach Ingalls Pass, stunning for its Mount Stuart and environs' views and the highest point of the trail.

Ingalls Lake is across the basin, about a mile-and-a-half away, hidden by a thousand boulders and reached only after passing through some heavenly parkland meadows. But first, drop down to the left following the trail as it picks its way down through boulder field and traces an arc contouring the inside of this Headlight Basin. (A route that drops almost straight down and might seem like a more direct route is one that actually leads to campsites; it eventually rejoins the arcing trail.)

Once through the rocks, enter heathery meadows and the occasional stand of trees, and find yourself in an idyllic setting passing gentle waterfalls, gentle tarns, gentle creeks—gentle everything— while gradually dropping about 300 feet of elevation. Soon the trail is not so gentle, and returns to its big blocky boulder phase, where you're scanning the rocks for cairns when the trail disappears. You'll use your hands as well as your feet in a couple of spots. Keep your eye out for the trail, though—it's there—and at **5.4** miles reach the lake, a rock-rimmed, azure pool so pristine and in such a spectacular

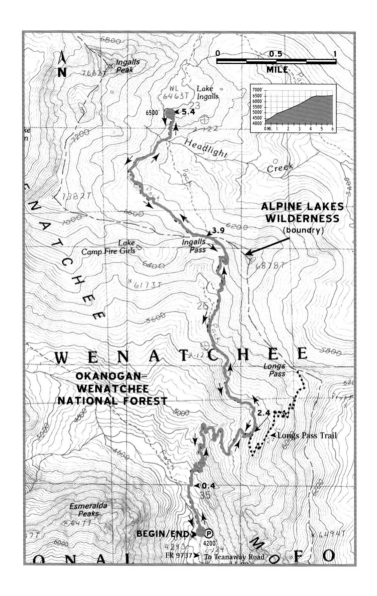

setting, it put me in mind of Oregon's mystical Crater Lake when I first saw it.

Mount Stuart and Jack Ridge rise high and reflect deeply in the lake to the east, with Ingalls Peak to the west. Plenty of rocks— down low, up high, and all around afford perfect spots for lunch and mountain-lake gazing.

Going Farther
The Longs Pass Trail (Hike 68) uses the same trailhead for 2.6 miles. Also, the Esmeralda Basin trail starts from the same trailhead. Camping is available at several campgrounds along Teanaway Road, the closest being Beverly Campground, about 4 miles before the trailhead on Forest Road 9737. ■

INDEX

ABOUT THE AUTHOR

MIKE MCQUAIDE has written outdoor, travel, and lifestyle stories for everyone from *Outside* and *Sunset* to *Runner's World*, *Adventure Cyclist*, and more. A former outdoors writer for the *Seattle Times*, Mike has written six books on outdoor recreation and travel including *Day Hike! North Cascades* and *75 Classic Rides: Washington*. He is also an avid cyclist—both road and mountain bike—as well as a trail runner, mountaineer, and snowboarder. He's been hiking and running Northwest trails for more than twenty-five years. Mike currently lives in Luxembourg with his wife, Jennifer, and son, Baker, named for the mountain. Follow his adventures at www.Facebook.com/AnAmericanInLuxembourg.